Mometrix
TEST PREPARATION

DSST®

Management Information Systems
Exam Secrets Study Guide

I0868259

DSST is a registered trademark of Prometric LLC, which is not affiliated with Mometrix Test Preparation and does not endorse this product.

DEAR FUTURE EXAM SUCCESS STORY

First of all, **THANK YOU** for purchasing Mometrix study materials!

Second, congratulations! You are one of the few determined test-takers who are committed to doing whatever it takes to excel on your exam. **You have come to the right place.** We developed these study materials with one goal in mind: to deliver you the information you need in a format that's concise and easy to use.

In addition to optimizing your guide for the content of the test, we've outlined our recommended steps for breaking down the preparation process into small, attainable goals so you can make sure you stay on track.

We've also analyzed the entire test-taking process, identifying the most common pitfalls and showing how you can overcome them and be ready for any curveball the test throws you.

Standardized testing is one of the biggest obstacles on your road to success, which only increases the importance of doing well in the high-pressure, high-stakes environment of test day. Your results on this test could have a significant impact on your future, and this guide provides the information and practical advice to help you achieve your full potential on test day.

Your success is our success

We would love to hear from you! If you would like to share the story of your exam success or if you have any questions or comments in regard to our products, please contact us at **800-673-8175** or **support@mometrix.com**.

Thanks again for your business and we wish you continued success!

Sincerely,
The Mometrix Test Preparation Team

Need more help? Check out our flashcards at:
http://MometrixFlashcards.com/DSST

Copyright © 2026 by Mometrix Media LLC. All rights reserved.
Written and edited by the Mometrix Exam Secrets Test Prep Team
Printed in the United States of America

TABLE OF CONTENTS

INTRODUCTION 1
SECRET KEY #1 – PLAN BIG, STUDY SMALL 2
SECRET KEY #2 – MAKE YOUR STUDYING COUNT 3
SECRET KEY #3 – PRACTICE THE RIGHT WAY 4
SECRET KEY #4 – PACE YOURSELF 6
SECRET KEY #5 – HAVE A PLAN FOR GUESSING 7
TEST-TAKING STRATEGIES 10
COMPUTER HARDWARE 15
COMPUTER SOFTWARE 20
TELECOMMUNICATIONS AND NETWORKS 25
BUSINESS INFORMATION SYSTEMS 34
SYSTEMS ANALYSIS AND DESIGN 42
MANAGING DATA RESOURCES 48
BUSINESS DECISION MAKING 55
MIS AND THE ORGANIZATION 61
MIS ISSUES 65
DSST PRACTICE TEST 70
ANSWER KEY AND EXPLANATIONS 72
HOW TO OVERCOME TEST ANXIETY 74
THANK YOU 80
ONLINE RESOURCES 81

Introduction

Thank you for purchasing this resource! You have made the choice to prepare yourself for a test that could have a huge impact on your future, and this guide is designed to help you be fully ready for test day. Obviously, it's important to have a solid understanding of the test material, but you also need to be prepared for the unique environment and stressors of the test, so that you can perform to the best of your abilities.

For this purpose, the first section that appears in this guide is the **Secret Keys**. We've devoted countless hours to meticulously researching what works and what doesn't, and we've boiled down our findings to the five most impactful steps you can take to improve your performance on the test. We start at the beginning with study planning and move through the preparation process, all the way to the testing strategies that will help you get the most out of what you know when you're finally sitting in front of the test.

We recommend that you start preparing for your test as far in advance as possible. However, if you've bought this guide as a last-minute study resource and only have a few days before your test, we recommend that you skip over the first two Secret Keys since they address a long-term study plan.

If you struggle with **test anxiety**, we strongly encourage you to check out our recommendations for how you can overcome it. Test anxiety is a formidable foe, but it can be beaten, and we want to make sure you have the tools you need to defeat it.

Copyright © Mometrix Media. You have been licensed one copy of this document for personal use only. Any other reproduction or redistribution is strictly prohibited. All rights reserved.
This content is provided for test preparation purposes only and does not imply an endorsement by Mometrix of any particular political, scientific, or religious point of view.

Secret Key #1 – Plan Big, Study Small

There's a lot riding on your performance. If you want to ace this test, you're going to need to keep your skills sharp and the material fresh in your mind. You need a plan that lets you review everything you need to know while still fitting in your schedule. We'll break this strategy down into three categories.

Information Organization

Start with the information you already have: the official test outline. From this, you can make a complete list of all the concepts you need to cover before the test. Organize these concepts into groups that can be studied together, and create a list of any related vocabulary you need to learn so you can brush up on any difficult terms. You'll want to keep this vocabulary list handy once you actually start studying since you may need to add to it along the way.

Time Management

Once you have your set of study concepts, decide how to spread them out over the time you have left before the test. Break your study plan into small, clear goals so you have a manageable task for each day and know exactly what you're doing. Then just focus on one small step at a time. When you manage your time this way, you don't need to spend hours at a time studying. Studying a small block of content for a short period each day helps you retain information better and avoid stressing over how much you have left to do. You can relax knowing that you have a plan to cover everything in time. In order for this strategy to be effective though, you have to start studying early and stick to your schedule. Avoid the exhaustion and futility that comes from last-minute cramming!

Study Environment

The environment you study in has a big impact on your learning. Studying in a coffee shop, while probably more enjoyable, is not likely to be as fruitful as studying in a quiet room. It's important to keep distractions to a minimum. You're only planning to study for a short block of time, so make the most of it. Don't pause to check your phone or get up to find a snack. It's also important to **avoid multitasking**. Research has consistently shown that multitasking will make your studying dramatically less effective. Your study area should also be comfortable and well-lit so you don't have the distraction of straining your eyes or sitting on an uncomfortable chair.

The time of day you study is also important. You want to be rested and alert. Don't wait until just before bedtime. Study when you'll be most likely to comprehend and remember. Even better, if you know what time of day your test will be, set that time aside for study. That way your brain will be used to working on that subject at that specific time and you'll have a better chance of recalling information.

Finally, it can be helpful to team up with others who are studying for the same test. Your actual studying should be done in as isolated an environment as possible, but the work of organizing the information and setting up the study plan can be divided up. In between study sessions, you can discuss with your teammates the concepts that you're all studying and quiz each other on the details. Just be sure that your teammates are as serious about the test as you are. If you find that your study time is being replaced with social time, you might need to find a new team.

Copyright © Mometrix Media. You have been licensed one copy of this document for personal use only. Any other reproduction or redistribution is strictly prohibited. All rights reserved.
This content is provided for test preparation purposes only and does not imply an endorsement by Mometrix of any particular political, scientific, or religious point of view.

Secret Key #2 – Make Your Studying Count

You're devoting a lot of time and effort to preparing for this test, so you want to be absolutely certain it will pay off. This means doing more than just reading the content and hoping you can remember it on test day. It's important to make every minute of study count. There are two main areas you can focus on to make your studying count.

Retention

It doesn't matter how much time you study if you can't remember the material. You need to make sure you are retaining the concepts. To check your retention of the information you're learning, try recalling it at later times with minimal prompting. Try carrying around flashcards and glance at one or two from time to time or ask a friend who's also studying for the test to quiz you.

To enhance your retention, look for ways to put the information into practice so that you can apply it rather than simply recalling it. If you're using the information in practical ways, it will be much easier to remember. Similarly, it helps to solidify a concept in your mind if you're not only reading it to yourself but also explaining it to someone else. Ask a friend to let you teach them about a concept you're a little shaky on (or speak aloud to an imaginary audience if necessary). As you try to summarize, define, give examples, and answer your friend's questions, you'll understand the concepts better and they will stay with you longer. Finally, step back for a big picture view and ask yourself how each piece of information fits with the whole subject. When you link the different concepts together and see them working together as a whole, it's easier to remember the individual components.

Finally, practice showing your work on any multi-step problems, even if you're just studying. Writing out each step you take to solve a problem will help solidify the process in your mind, and you'll be more likely to remember it during the test.

Modality

Modality simply refers to the means or method by which you study. Choosing a study modality that fits your own individual learning style is crucial. No two people learn best in exactly the same way, so it's important to know your strengths and use them to your advantage.

For example, if you learn best by visualization, focus on visualizing a concept in your mind and draw an image or a diagram. Try color-coding your notes, illustrating them, or creating symbols that will trigger your mind to recall a learned concept. If you learn best by hearing or discussing information, find a study partner who learns the same way or read aloud to yourself. Think about how to put the information in your own words. Imagine that you are giving a lecture on the topic and record yourself so you can listen to it later.

For any learning style, flashcards can be helpful. Organize the information so you can take advantage of spare moments to review. Underline key words or phrases. Use different colors for different categories. Mnemonic devices (such as creating a short list in which every item starts with the same letter) can also help with retention. Find what works best for you and use it to store the information in your mind most effectively and easily.

Copyright © Mometrix Media. You have been licensed one copy of this document for personal use only. Any other reproduction or redistribution is strictly prohibited. All rights reserved.
This content is provided for test preparation purposes only and does not imply an endorsement by Mometrix of any particular political, scientific, or religious point of view.

Secret Key #3 – Practice the Right Way

Your success on test day depends not only on how many hours you put into preparing, but also on whether you prepared the right way. It's good to check along the way to see if your studying is paying off. One of the most effective ways to do this is by taking practice tests to evaluate your progress. Practice tests are useful because they show exactly where you need to improve. Every time you take a practice test, pay special attention to these three groups of questions:

- The questions you got wrong
- The questions you had to guess on, even if you guessed right
- The questions you found difficult or slow to work through

This will show you exactly what your weak areas are, and where you need to devote more study time. Ask yourself why each of these questions gave you trouble. Was it because you didn't understand the material? Was it because you didn't remember the vocabulary? Do you need more repetitions on this type of question to build speed and confidence? Dig into those questions and figure out how you can strengthen your weak areas as you go back to review the material.

Additionally, many practice tests have a section explaining the answer choices. It can be tempting to read the explanation and think that you now have a good understanding of the concept. However, an explanation likely only covers part of the question's broader context. Even if the explanation makes perfect sense, **go back and investigate** every concept related to the question until you're positive you have a thorough understanding.

As you go along, keep in mind that the practice test is just that: practice. Memorizing these questions and answers will not be very helpful on the actual test because it is unlikely to have any of the same exact questions. If you only know the right answers to the sample questions, you won't be prepared for the real thing. **Study the concepts** until you understand them fully, and then you'll be able to answer any question that shows up on the test.

It's important to wait on the practice tests until you're ready. If you take a test on your first day of study, you may be overwhelmed by the amount of material covered and how much you need to learn. Work up to it gradually.

On test day, you'll need to be prepared for answering questions, managing your time, and using the test-taking strategies you've learned. It's a lot to balance, like a mental marathon that will have a big impact on your future. Like training for a marathon, you'll need to start slowly and work your way up. When test day arrives, you'll be ready.

Start with the strategies you've read in the first two Secret Keys—plan your course and study in the way that works best for you. If you have time, consider using multiple study resources to get different approaches to the same concepts. It can be helpful to see difficult concepts from more than one angle. Then find a good source for practice tests. Many times, the test website will suggest potential study resources or provide sample tests.

Copyright © Mometrix Media. You have been licensed one copy of this document for personal use only. Any other reproduction or redistribution is strictly prohibited. All rights reserved.
This content is provided for test preparation purposes only and does not imply an endorsement by Mometrix of any particular political, scientific, or religious point of view.

Practice Test Strategy

If you're able to find at least three practice tests, we recommend this strategy:

Untimed and Open-Book Practice

Take the first test with no time constraints and with your notes and study guide handy. Take your time and focus on applying the strategies you've learned.

Timed and Open-Book Practice

Take the second practice test open-book as well, but set a timer and practice pacing yourself to finish in time.

Timed and Closed-Book Practice

Take any other practice tests as if it were test day. Set a timer and put away your study materials. Sit at a table or desk in a quiet room, imagine yourself at the testing center, and answer questions as quickly and accurately as possible.

Keep repeating timed and closed-book tests on a regular basis until you run out of practice tests or it's time for the actual test. Your mind will be ready for the schedule and stress of test day, and you'll be able to focus on recalling the material you've learned.

Copyright © Mometrix Media. You have been licensed one copy of this document for personal use only. Any other reproduction or redistribution is strictly prohibited. All rights reserved.
This content is provided for test preparation purposes only and does not imply an endorsement by Mometrix of any particular political, scientific, or religious point of view.

Secret Key #4 – Pace Yourself

Once you're fully prepared for the material on the test, your biggest challenge on test day will be managing your time. Just knowing that the clock is ticking can make you panic even if you have plenty of time left. Work on pacing yourself so you can build confidence against the time constraints of the exam. Pacing is a difficult skill to master, especially in a high-pressure environment, so **practice is vital**.

Set time expectations for your pace based on how much time is available. For example, if a section has 60 questions and the time limit is 30 minutes, you know you have to average 30 seconds or less per question in order to answer them all. Although 30 seconds is the hard limit, set 25 seconds per question as your goal, so you reserve extra time to spend on harder questions. When you budget extra time for the harder questions, you no longer have any reason to stress when those questions take longer to answer.

Don't let this time expectation distract you from working through the test at a calm, steady pace, but keep it in mind so you don't spend too much time on any one question. Recognize that taking extra time on one question you don't understand may keep you from answering two that you do understand later in the test. If your time limit for a question is up and you're still not sure of the answer, mark it and move on, and come back to it later if the time and the test format allow. If the testing format doesn't allow you to return to earlier questions, just make an educated guess; then put it out of your mind and move on.

On the easier questions, be careful not to rush. It may seem wise to hurry through them so you have more time for the challenging ones, but it's not worth missing one if you know the concept and just didn't take the time to read the question fully. Work efficiently but make sure you understand the question and have looked at all of the answer choices, since more than one may seem right at first.

Even if you're paying attention to the time, you may find yourself a little behind at some point. You should speed up to get back on track, but do so wisely. Don't panic; just take a few seconds less on each question until you're caught up. Don't guess without thinking, but do look through the answer choices and eliminate any you know are wrong. If you can get down to two choices, it is often worthwhile to guess from those. Once you've chosen an answer, move on and don't dwell on any that you skipped or had to hurry through. If a question was taking too long, chances are it was one of the harder ones, so you weren't as likely to get it right anyway.

On the other hand, if you find yourself getting ahead of schedule, it may be beneficial to slow down a little. The more quickly you work, the more likely you are to make a careless mistake that will affect your score. You've budgeted time for each question, so don't be afraid to spend that time. Practice an efficient but careful pace to get the most out of the time you have.

Copyright © Mometrix Media. You have been licensed one copy of this document for personal use only. Any other reproduction or redistribution is strictly prohibited. All rights reserved.
This content is provided for test preparation purposes only and does not imply an endorsement by Mometrix of any particular political, scientific, or religious point of view.

Secret Key #5 – Have a Plan for Guessing

When you're taking the test, you may find yourself stuck on a question. Some of the answer choices seem better than others, but you don't see the one answer choice that is obviously correct. What do you do?

The scenario described above is very common, yet most test takers have not effectively prepared for it. Developing and practicing a plan for guessing may be one of the single most effective uses of your time as you get ready for the exam.

In developing your plan for guessing, there are three questions to address:

- When should you start the guessing process?
- How should you narrow down the choices?
- Which answer should you choose?

When to Start the Guessing Process

Unless your plan for guessing is to select C every time (which, despite its merits, is not what we recommend), you need to leave yourself enough time to apply your answer elimination strategies. Since you have a limited amount of time for each question, that means that if you're going to give yourself the best shot at guessing correctly, you have to decide quickly whether or not you will guess.

Of course, the best-case scenario is that you don't have to guess at all, so first, see if you can answer the question based on your knowledge of the subject and basic reasoning skills. Focus on the key words in the question and try to jog your memory of related topics. Give yourself a chance to bring the knowledge to mind, but once you realize that you don't have (or you can't access) the knowledge you need to answer the question, it's time to start the guessing process.

It's almost always better to start the guessing process too early than too late. It only takes a few seconds to remember something and answer the question from knowledge. Carefully eliminating wrong answer choices takes longer. Plus, going through the process of eliminating answer choices can actually help jog your memory.

Summary: Start the guessing process as soon as you decide that you can't answer the question based on your knowledge.

Copyright © Mometrix Media. You have been licensed one copy of this document for personal use only. Any other reproduction or redistribution is strictly prohibited. All rights reserved.
This content is provided for test preparation purposes only and does not imply an endorsement by Mometrix of any particular political, scientific, or religious point of view.

How to Narrow Down the Choices

The next chapter in this book (**Test-Taking Strategies**) includes a wide range of strategies for how to approach questions and how to look for answer choices to eliminate. You will definitely want to read those carefully, practice them, and figure out which ones work best for you. Here though, we're going to address a mindset rather than a particular strategy.

Your odds of guessing an answer correctly depend on how many options you are choosing from.

Number of options left	5	4	3	2	1
Odds of guessing correctly	20%	25%	33%	50%	100%

You can see from this chart just how valuable it is to be able to eliminate incorrect answers and make an educated guess, but there are two things that many test takers do that cause them to miss out on the benefits of guessing:

- Accidentally eliminating the correct answer
- Selecting an answer based on an impression

We'll look at the first one here, and the second one in the next section.

To avoid accidentally eliminating the correct answer, we recommend a thought exercise called **the $5 challenge**. In this challenge, you only eliminate an answer choice from contention if you are willing to bet $5 on it being wrong. Why $5? Five dollars is a small but not insignificant amount of money. It's an amount you could afford to lose but wouldn't want to throw away. And while losing $5 once might not hurt too much, doing it twenty times will set you back $100. In the same way, each small decision you make—eliminating a choice here, guessing on a question there—won't by itself impact your score very much, but when you put them all together, they can make a big difference. By holding each answer choice elimination decision to a higher standard, you can reduce the risk of accidentally eliminating the correct answer.

The $5 challenge can also be applied in a positive sense: If you are willing to bet $5 that an answer choice *is* correct, go ahead and mark it as correct.

Summary: Only eliminate an answer choice if you are willing to bet $5 that it is wrong.

Copyright © Mometrix Media. You have been licensed one copy of this document for personal use only. Any other reproduction or redistribution is strictly prohibited. All rights reserved.
This content is provided for test preparation purposes only and does not imply an endorsement by Mometrix of any particular political, scientific, or religious point of view.

Which Answer to Choose

You're taking the test. You've run into a hard question and decided you'll have to guess. You've eliminated all the answer choices you're willing to bet $5 on. Now you have to pick an answer. Why do we even need to talk about this? Why can't you just pick whichever one you feel like when the time comes?

The answer to these questions is that if you don't come into the test with a plan, you'll rely on your impression to select an answer choice, and if you do that, you risk falling into a trap. The test writers know that everyone who takes their test will be guessing on some of the questions, so they intentionally write wrong answer choices to seem plausible. You still have to pick an answer though, and if the wrong answer choices are designed to look right, how can you ever be sure that you're not falling for their trap? The best solution we've found to this dilemma is to take the decision out of your hands entirely. Here is the process we recommend:

Once you've eliminated any choices that you are confident (willing to bet $5) are wrong, select the first remaining choice as your answer.

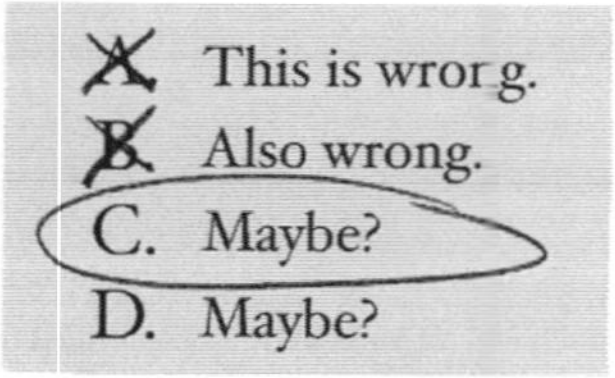

Whether you choose to select the first remaining choice, the second, or the last, the important thing is that you use some preselected standard. Using this approach guarantees that you will not be enticed into selecting an answer choice that looks right, because you are not basing your decision on how the answer choices look.

This is not meant to make you question your knowledge. Instead, it is to help you recognize the difference between your knowledge and your impressions. There's a huge difference between thinking an answer is right because of what you know, and thinking an answer is right because it looks or sounds like it should be right.

Summary: To ensure that your selection is appropriately random, make a predetermined selection from among all answer choices you have not eliminated.

Copyright © Mometrix Media. You have been licensed one copy of this document for personal use only. Any other reproduction or redistribution is strictly prohibited. All rights reserved.
This content is provided for test preparation purposes only and does not imply an endorsement by Mometrix of any particular political, scientific, or religious point of view.

Test-Taking Strategies

This section contains a list of test-taking strategies that you may find helpful as you work through the test. By taking what you know and applying logical thought, you can maximize your chances of answering any question correctly!

It is very important to realize that every question is different and every person is different: no single strategy will work on every question, and no single strategy will work for every person. That's why we've included all of them here, so you can try them out and determine which ones work best for different types of questions and which ones work best for you.

Question Strategies

✓ Read Carefully

Read the question and the answer choices carefully. Don't miss the question because you misread the terms. You have plenty of time to read each question thoroughly and make sure you understand what is being asked. Yet a happy medium must be attained, so don't waste too much time. You must read carefully and efficiently.

✓ Contextual Clues

Look for contextual clues. If the question includes a word you are not familiar with, look at the immediate context for some indication of what the word might mean. Contextual clues can often give you all the information you need to decipher the meaning of an unfamiliar word. Even if you can't determine the meaning, you may be able to narrow down the possibilities enough to make a solid guess at the answer to the question.

✓ Prefixes

If you're having trouble with a word in the question or answer choices, try dissecting it. Take advantage of every clue that the word might include. Prefixes can be a huge help. Usually, they allow you to determine a basic meaning. *Pre-* means before, *post-* means after, *pro-* is positive, *de-* is negative. From prefixes, you can get an idea of the general meaning of the word and try to put it into context.

✓ Hedge Words

Watch out for critical hedge words, such as *likely, may, can, often, almost, mostly, usually, generally, rarely*, and *sometimes*. Question writers insert these hedge phrases to cover every possibility. Often an answer choice will be wrong simply because it leaves no room for exception. Be on guard for answer choices that have definitive words such as *exactly* and *always*.

✓ Switchback Words

Stay alert for *switchbacks*. These are the words and phrases frequently used to alert you to shifts in thought. The most common switchback words are *but, although*, and *however*. Others include *nevertheless, on the other hand, even though, while, in spite of, despite*, and *regardless of*. Switchback words are important to catch because they can change the direction of the question or an answer choice.

Copyright © Mometrix Media. You have been licensed one copy of this document for personal use only. Any other reproduction or redistribution is strictly prohibited. All rights reserved.
This content is provided for test preparation purposes only and does not imply an endorsement by Mometrix of any particular political, scientific, or religious point of view.

☑ FACE VALUE

When in doubt, use common sense. Accept the situation in the problem at face value. Don't read too much into it. These problems will not require you to make wild assumptions. If you have to go beyond creativity and warp time or space in order to have an answer choice fit the question, then you should move on and consider the other answer choices. These are normal problems rooted in reality. The applicable relationship or explanation may not be readily apparent, but it is there for you to figure out. Use your common sense to interpret anything that isn't clear.

Answer Choice Strategies

☑ ANSWER SELECTION

The most thorough way to pick an answer choice is to identify and eliminate wrong answers until only one is left, then confirm it is the correct answer. Sometimes an answer choice may immediately seem right, but be careful. The test writers will usually put more than one reasonable answer choice on each question, so take a second to read all of them and make sure that the other choices are not equally obvious. As long as you have time left, it is better to read every answer choice than to pick the first one that looks right without checking the others.

☑ ANSWER CHOICE FAMILIES

An answer choice family consists of two (in rare cases, three) answer choices that are very similar in construction and cannot all be true at the same time. If you see two answer choices that are direct opposites or parallels, one of them is usually the correct answer. For instance, if one answer choice says that quantity *x* increases and another either says that quantity *x* decreases (opposite) or says that quantity *y* increases (parallel), then those answer choices would fall into the same family. An answer choice that doesn't match the construction of the answer choice family is more likely to be incorrect. Most questions will not have answer choice families, but when they do appear, you should be prepared to recognize them.

☑ ELIMINATE ANSWERS

Eliminate answer choices as soon as you realize they are wrong, but make sure you consider all possibilities. If you are eliminating answer choices and realize that the last one you are left with is also wrong, don't panic. Start over and consider each choice again. There may be something you missed the first time that you will realize on the second pass.

☑ AVOID FACT TRAPS

Don't be distracted by an answer choice that is factually true but doesn't answer the question. You are looking for the choice that answers the question. Stay focused on what the question is asking for so you don't accidentally pick an answer that is true but incorrect. Always go back to the question and make sure the answer choice you've selected actually answers the question and is not merely a true statement.

☑ EXTREME STATEMENTS

In general, you should avoid answers that put forth extreme actions as standard practice or proclaim controversial ideas as established fact. An answer choice that states the "process should be used in certain situations, if..." is much more likely to be correct than one that states the "process should be discontinued completely." The first is a calm rational statement and doesn't even make a definitive, uncompromising stance, using a hedge word *if* to provide wiggle room, whereas the second choice is far more extreme.

Copyright © Mometrix Media. You have been licensed one copy of this document for personal use only. Any other reproduction or redistribution is strictly prohibited. All rights reserved.
This content is provided for test preparation purposes only and does not imply an endorsement by Mometrix of any particular political, scientific, or religious point of view.

☑ BENCHMARK

As you read through the answer choices and you come across one that seems to answer the question well, mentally select that answer choice. This is not your final answer, but it's the one that will help you evaluate the other answer choices. The one that you selected is your benchmark or standard for judging each of the other answer choices. Every other answer choice must be compared to your benchmark. That choice is correct until proven otherwise by another answer choice beating it. If you find a better answer, then that one becomes your new benchmark. Once you've decided that no other choice answers the question as well as your benchmark, you have your final answer.

☑ PREDICT THE ANSWER

Before you even start looking at the answer choices, it is often best to try to predict the answer. When you come up with the answer on your own, it is easier to avoid distractions and traps because you will know exactly what to look for. The right answer choice is unlikely to be word-for-word what you came up with, but it should be a close match. Even if you are confident that you have the right answer, you should still take the time to read each option before moving on.

General Strategies

☑ TOUGH QUESTIONS

If you are stumped on a problem or it appears too hard or too difficult, don't waste time. Move on! Remember though, if you can quickly check for obviously incorrect answer choices, your chances of guessing correctly are greatly improved. Before you completely give up, at least try to knock out a couple of possible answers. Eliminate what you can and then guess at the remaining answer choices before moving on.

☑ CHECK YOUR WORK

Since you will probably not know every term listed and the answer to every question, it is important that you get credit for the ones that you do know. Don't miss any questions through careless mistakes. If at all possible, try to take a second to look back over your answer selection and make sure you've selected the correct answer choice and haven't made a costly careless mistake (such as marking an answer choice that you didn't mean to mark). This quick double check should more than pay for itself in caught mistakes for the time it costs.

☑ PACE YOURSELF

It's easy to be overwhelmed when you're looking at a page full of questions; your mind is confused and full of random thoughts, and the clock is ticking down faster than you would like. Calm down and maintain the pace that you have set for yourself. Especially as you get down to the last few minutes of the test, don't let the small numbers on the clock make you panic. As long as you are on track by monitoring your pace, you are guaranteed to have time for each question.

☑ DON'T RUSH

It is very easy to make errors when you are in a hurry. Maintaining a fast pace in answering questions is pointless if it makes you miss questions that you would have gotten right otherwise. Test writers like to include distracting information and wrong answers that seem right. Taking a little extra time to avoid careless mistakes can make all the difference in your test score. Find a pace that allows you to be confident in the answers that you select.

Copyright © Mometrix Media. You have been licensed one copy of this document for personal use only. Any other reproduction or redistribution is strictly prohibited. All rights reserved.
This content is provided for test preparation purposes only and does not imply an endorsement by Mometrix of any particular political, scientific, or religious point of view.

⊘ KEEP MOVING

Panicking will not help you pass the test, so do your best to stay calm and keep moving. Taking deep breaths and going through the answer elimination steps you practiced can help to break through a stress barrier and keep your pace.

Final Notes

The combination of a solid foundation of content knowledge and the confidence that comes from practicing your plan for applying that knowledge is the key to maximizing your performance on test day. As your foundation of content knowledge is built up and strengthened, you'll find that the strategies included in this chapter become more and more effective in helping you quickly sift through the distractions and traps of the test to isolate the correct answer.

Now that you're preparing to move forward into the test content chapters of this book, be sure to keep your goal in mind. As you read, think about how you will be able to apply this information on the test. If you've already seen sample questions for the test and you have an idea of the question format and style, try to come up with questions of your own that you can answer based on what you're reading. This will give you valuable practice applying your knowledge in the same ways you can expect to on test day.

Good luck and good studying!

Copyright © Mometrix Media. You have been licensed one copy of this document for personal use only. Any other reproduction or redistribution is strictly prohibited. All rights reserved.
This content is provided for test preparation purposes only and does not imply an endorsement by Mometrix of any particular political, scientific, or religious point of view.

Copyright © Mometrix Media. You have been licensed one copy of this document for personal use only. Any other reproduction or redistribution is strictly prohibited. All rights reserved.
This content is provided for test preparation purposes only and does not imply an endorsement by Mometrix of any particular political, scientific, or religious point of view.

Computer Hardware

Utilitarian Approach to Ethical Issues

In a utilitarian approach, the right thing to do is what produces the most good ("utility") for the greatest number of people. So, utilitarian's focus on the likely consequences of actions to assess the ethical merits of those actions. In business settings, a utilitarian approach often focuses on what is good for the people involved with a company (such as employees, managers, and shareholders). For instance, when deciding whether to use money to limit a company's air emissions or to increase employee wages, a utilitarian might conclude it is better to spend the money on pay increases (perhaps employees are likely to be happier with additional income than with marginally better air quality). A challenge for this view is that it does not take into account the consequences of an action for everyone affected by that action (all the people who breathe the air near the company, for instance).

ENIAC and the UNIVAC I

The first machine that can be defined as a computer was developed in 1946 at the University of Pennsylvania. Engineers John W. Mauchly and J. Presper Eckert developed the Electronic Numerical Integrator and Calculator, or ENIAC.

The ENIAC led to development of the UNIVAC 1, from Remington Rand. This computer entered the marketplace in 1951, when the first machine was installed at the US Census Bureau. In 1954, General Electric acquired a UNIVAC as well, the first business to use a computer.

Compared to today's computers, these early versions were quite slow, performing fewer than 2,000 calculations per second. Today's least powerful computers can perform more than 2 billion calculations per second.

IBM's System/360 Computer Line

Throughout the 1950s, massive computer systems focused on a single task continued to be the mainstay of the computer market. IBM entered the computer manufacturing fray later than some other companies, but quickly developed a full line of computing products.

In the 1960s, IBM's innovations led to the arrival of the System/360 computers. Rather than responding to a single user, these computers could perform tasks requested by many users. Although a computer processor can actually handle only one processing request at a time, the System/360 could process part of one request, then move on to another, and continue in this manner to complete multiple processes one step at a time in a quick and efficient manner. Previously, each individual process had to be requested and completed before another process could begin.

The System/360 line was highly innovative and a huge step forward in computer hardware development these computers were costly and only the largest companies were able to afford and make use of them.

"Mini" and "Micro" Computers

As more business functions became dependent on the use of computers, it became tiresome and time-consuming to have to funnel all computer-related activity through information specialists who were trained to handle the machines. Seeing a demand for more individualized computers,

Copyright © Mometrix Media. You have been licensed one copy of this document for personal use only. Any other reproduction or redistribution is strictly prohibited. All rights reserved.
This content is provided for test preparation purposes only and does not imply an endorsement by Mometrix of any particular political, scientific, or religious point of view.

companies began to develop smaller, more compact machines. These computers were aimed at meeting the needs of small organizations.

The minicomputer led quickly to the microcomputer, intended for use by an individual, or even for home use. Apple and Tandy pioneered the microcomputer, but the idea of the personal computer took off when IBM introduced the personal computer, or PC, in 1982. The term "PC" has become universal in referring to a small computer meant for individual use.

PC DEVELOPMENT

Since the development of the first personal computers in the 1980s, the PC has rapidly grown and improved. Current PCs are exponentially faster and more powerful than these early models.

Apple's work in pioneering the microcomputer led to increased market share early in the computer's development. The Apple computer's usability led Microsoft to develop the Windows operating system, with a look and feel similar to Apple's efforts. Because these PCs, then referred to as "IBM-compatible" machines, were less expensive than the arguably better-quality Apple machines, they quickly took away market share from Apple. In recent years, Apple has recaptured a significant portion of the market, though the Windows PC remains more common in business environments.

MOORE'S LAW

Moore's Law states that the storage capacity of a single silicon chip doubles every year. The saying originated in the 1960s and was named for a founder of the Intel Corporation, Gordon Moore. Intel specializes in manufacturing processor chips.

By the 1970s, Moore's Law was already obsolete, as growth slowed such that the capacity of a chip doubled about every year and a half. This rate continues today, and must be considered when planning computer system purchases for a business. Every 18 months, the computer sitting on any individual's desk can be replaced for the same cost by a computer that is twice as powerful. While less powerful computers can continue to be useful, at some point they are no longer able to handle the increasingly greater demands put on them by improved software and hardware.

MAINFRAME

The term "mainframe" originally referred to the computer itself. Early computers accomplished one task at a time and were used by a single person. Today's mainframes are large computers usually accessed by a large number of people. A large modern business often has a centrally located mainframe computer that is accessible by numerous users throughout the company. These large computers are sometimes comparable in size to the original, single-machine "mainframes," but they can handle much larger quantities of data and processing functions.

MULTITASKING

Although a computer technically can handle only one process at a time, multitasking allows multiple processes to be interspersed with each other. The computer automatically allocates its resources to efficiently combine different requested tasks. A part of one process is finished, then the computer will do a part of another task, then go back to the first task, et cetera, in such a way that its resources are most efficiently allocated to complete all the requested processing tasks in the least possible amount of time. The System/360 computers from IBM, developed in the 1960s, were the first with this ability.

In the case of multiple users, a computer equipped for multitasking will also be able to determine when two or more users are attempting to perform contradictory tasks. In this case, the computer

Copyright © Mometrix Media. You have been licensed one copy of this document for personal use only. Any other reproduction or redistribution is strictly prohibited. All rights reserved.
This content is provided for test preparation purposes only and does not imply an endorsement by Mometrix of any particular political, scientific, or religious point of view.

will lock out one user's tasks until the task that was requested first has been completed. This prevents duplicated or contradictory data.

Information Specialist

Early computers required specially trained individuals to program them for individual required processes. Any time a function needed to be handled by a computer, those requesting the procedure would pass the request through the information specialist. Only one request could be managed at a time due to the processing limitations of early computers. Because of this, requests often became backlogged, leaving employees impatiently waiting for vital information or for important tasks to be completed. With the advent of minicomputers and microcomputers, as well as the personal computer, computers became much less expensive and much easier for individuals to use. This allowed individual employees or organizations to request and handle their own information tasks. It also led to the proliferation of computers for home use.

IT Specialist

Today, various computer maintenance functions are handled by an information technology (IT) specialist or an IT department in an individual business. These departments or individuals ensure that computers are working at optimal functionality. They maintain hardware and software, ensure updated and efficient network security, and often maintain large servers to which a large number of individual computers are connected. The job of IT specialist is in high demand in today's business world. Larger companies almost always maintain a full-time IT staff, while smaller companies will often employ a single IT specialist or outsource the work on a contract basis to a company that performs this function for a variety of companies or even individuals.

Computer Hardware

Computers require hardware to perform four major functions, these functions are:

- *Input*: One portion of the computer must handle data that is input into the machine. This input is typically supplied by the user
- *Processing*: Another portion must process that input and produce the desired output. For example, the computer receives specific input from a piece of graphics software and processes this to produce the desired result, which is a modification of an existing graphic accomplished by manipulating the data depicted by that graphic
- *Output*: One of the physical components of the computer must produce the output in a form that the user can easily interpret, such as the visual representation of a graphic
- *Secondary storage*: The computer needs a place to store all the data, whether it is being used or not. This can be accomplished through an internal hard drive built into the computer as well as through a variety of external storage devices

Computer Processor

The processor is the fastest functioning component of the computer. Processor function is measured in nanoseconds, which are billionths of a second. Because the processor is so fast, it can hold data in a cache and release it as it is needed by the slower components. The overall speed and performance capability of any computer is dependent on the speed of the processor.

Several different companies produce computer processors, and each company structures the processor slightly differently. For example, an Intel processor, common in Windows-based computers, is slightly different from processors designed for older Macintosh computers, which are usually made by Motorola (newer Macintosh computers use Intel processors or a combination of

Copyright © Mometrix Media. You have been licensed one copy of this document for personal use only. Any other reproduction or redistribution is strictly prohibited. All rights reserved.
This content is provided for test preparation purposes only and does not imply an endorsement by Mometrix of any particular political, scientific, or religious point of view.

Intel and Motorola). Some companies make "clone" processors designed to be compatible with chips made by the major manufacturers.

Input Devices

Input devices allow a user to interact directly with the computer. There are many input devices available, and users make use of different devices depending on the work they are doing.

The keyboard and mouse are the most commonly used input devices. The keyboard allows a user to input alphanumeric data such as text into a word processor. The mouse provides a simple interface to execute commands such as opening a program or performing tasks within a piece of software. Before the mouse became common, all commands had to be entered into the computer with keyboard commands.

Other input devices include scanners, touch screens, pen devices, microphones to capture sound, and speech-recognition and video-capture devices.

Output Devices

The most necessary and common output device is the monitor. The monitor produces a visual representation of the data being processed within the computer. To produce this output, the computer must be equipped with a video card. Different types of video cards produce different quality levels of video output. For example, if a computer is used frequently to view high-definition video or for gaming applications, a higher-quality, faster video card is necessary for acceptable performance. A variety of monitors exist today, from earlier cathode ray tube monitors to newer flat-screen monitors and heads-up displays.

Printers are also a very commonly used output device. Printers produce a hard copy on paper of the data that has been processed. There are many kinds of printers, from inexpensive ink-jet printers to costly printers designed for press-quality output.

Secondary Storage

The most common type of secondary storage is the computer's hard drive. The hard drive within the computer is a mechanical drive that spins and requires read/write heads to copy and interpret data. The size of the internal hard drive determines how much data an individual computer can store. Pre-Windows PCs functioned with as little as 40 megabytes of hard drive space. Today's computers are more likely to carry an internal hard drive of one hundred or more gigabytes.

External, portable data storage is very popular as well. USB drives are useful for data that must be carried quickly and easily from one computer to another. While PCs originally allowed data to be written to floppy discs, this functionality has been replaced by USB drives or memory sticks as well as writable CDs and DVDs. These formats are much more stable and long-lasting than the old floppy discs.

Motherboard

A computer's motherboard is the main circuit board within the computer. It ensures that the various components within the computer work together properly. The CPU or central processing unit, RAM (random access memory), and ROM (read-only memory, or storage memory) all coordinate through the motherboard.

The motherboard also contains circuitry to help input devices function properly. The keyboard, mouse, USB ports, and CD and/or DVD drives are also controlled through the motherboard. It also connects to expansion slots for additional RAM.

Copyright © Mometrix Media. You have been licensed one copy of this document for personal use only. Any other reproduction or redistribution is strictly prohibited. All rights reserved.
This content is provided for test preparation purposes only and does not imply an endorsement by Mometrix of any particular political, scientific, or religious point of view.

Without the motherboard, the computer cannot function. It is possible, and not uncommon, for the motherboard to stop functioning without damaging the data in the computer's memory.

TWO PERSONAL COMPUTING DEVICES

The proliferation of personal computing devices—small devices that provide computing power, Internet access, and other important functionality—is changing the way many companies do business. Among these devices are:

- *Multifunctional cell phones*: The cell phone has recently become the personal device of choice for many users. Even the most basic cell phone models now include the ability to text and access the Internet. They also maintain contact lists and to-do lists, and perform other productivity functions
- *Smart phones*: The smart phone can do nearly anything a small computer can. It can make and receive calls, surf the Internet through a built-in browser, play and record video, take photos, and use small applications that allow a myriad of productivity and record-keeping functions

RAM AND ROM

RAM stands for random access memory. Basically, RAM defines the amount of memory available on the computer's motherboard. This memory is used as a cache of sorts to increase the efficiency of the computer's processing functions. When the computer is powered down, RAM memory is cleared.

ROM is read-only memory, or fixed storage. This defines the amount of data a computer can store permanently for access when needed. Any application installed on the computer takes up a certain amount of ROM, as do files of any type. This type of memory is not cleared out unless the user deletes items.

PRINTERS

The two major types of printers are ink-jet printers and laser printers.

The ink-jet printer is usually less expensive and smaller than the laser printer. An ink-jet printer works by spraying tiny amounts of ink onto the paper. Even the least expensive ink-jet printers can provide clean, high-resolution color output. Ink-jet machines tend to be fairly slow. Multi-use ink-jet printers can also function as copiers, fax machines, and scanners.

Laser printers work much more quickly, but are more expensive and usually larger. Color printing on a laser printer adds significantly to the cost. A laser printer works similarly to a copy machine, and often doubles as a copier and scanner.

In both cases, higher resolution will lead to slower printing speeds and higher costs.

Copyright © Mometrix Media. You have been licensed one copy of this document for personal use only. Any other reproduction or redistribution is strictly prohibited. All rights reserved.
This content is provided for test preparation purposes only and does not imply an endorsement by Mometrix of any particular political, scientific, or religious point of view.

Computer Software

Programmed Computers

Original computer programming involved reorganizing connections between various pieces of hardware. Programmers had to physically move wires from place to place, connecting hardware together in different configurations to accomplish the end result.

As hardware changed and became more sophisticated, programming began to consist of data input directly into the processor. Programming languages were developed that could issue discrete orders to the processor. These collections of orders gradually became more sophisticated becoming the advanced computer-programming languages we are familiar with today.

Punch-Card Programming

One early way to deliver programming information to computer systems was via punch cards. These were flexible cards encoded with data. Each card could hold 80 characters of data. Only 72 of those were available for programming data; the others held other data such as sequencing information for individual cards. Full programs consisted of decks of cards that were fed into the computer through a card reader. Programmers kept boxes of job decks for collections of individual programs.

This type of programming was used in nearly all IBM computers. Languages such as FORTRAN and COBOL operated with punch cards. Other programming methods began to take over in the mid-80s.

Text-Based and Graphics-Based Software

As programming became more sophisticated, so did computer programs. Most programs, particularly for IBM and IBM-compatible computers, were text-based, meaning that text input was required from the keyboard to perform commands. The DOS system, a Microsoft operating system popular through this period, required the user to view the directory trees on the drive and issue commands to navigate through the data stored on the computer.

Graphics-based software gives the user a visual representation of the stored data, using icons to represent drives and folders as well as individual programs and documents. This led to a movement away from keyboard input to input via a mouse, particularly when navigating through the operating system and individual applications.

IBM-Compatible vs. Early Macintosh

Graphical interfaces were used early on in the development of Apple computers, while IBM-compatible systems remained text-based. The user had to learn specific text commands to navigate through the operating system as well as through stored files, and to execute applications.

The graphical user interfaces favored by the Apple operating systems proved more popular with users. They were easier to use, as they required the user only to select a graphic rather than having to remember a group of text commands. This approach to navigation was eventually adopted by formerly MS-DOS-based PCs with the arrival of the Windows operating system. DOS commands are still used by some for various maintenance functions within Windows.

Windows OS

The first version of the Windows OS (operating system) arrived in 1985, when Microsoft developed this graphical user interface (GUI) for its MS-DOS operating system. Many elements of the user

Copyright © Mometrix Media. You have been licensed one copy of this document for personal use only. Any other reproduction or redistribution is strictly prohibited. All rights reserved.
This content is provided for test preparation purposes only and does not imply an endorsement by Mometrix of any particular political, scientific, or religious point of view.

interface developed from work Microsoft had done in conjunction with Apple. Over the next few years, this GUI developed into a full operating system.

Windows did not really take off as an OS until 1990, with the arrival of Windows 3.0. Continued improvements in the system, as well as moves into other portions of the market, such as LAN operating systems, saw Microsoft's Windows OS becoming the predominant OS in the PC marketplace, eclipsing IBM's formerly popular OS/2 and Apple/Macintosh OSs, which were limited to Apple computers. This trend continues, although Apple has seen its market share increase again in recent years.

Microsoft Operating Systems Prevalence

There are several reasons why the Microsoft Windows OS is so prevalent in today's workplace. A major reason is that Windows is portable to a variety of different brands and types of computers that are all based on the old IBM-compatible model. Businesses are not limited to a particular brand of computer to use Windows, allowing them more options as regards pricing and computer power.

By contrast, the Apple-based OS is specific to Apple Macintosh computers. These computers are perceived to be less flexible and more expensive than Windows-based computers, though this is in many ways an inaccurate assumption. In recent years, the rising popularity of the Apple brand and the unpopularity of the latest Windows OS options (e.g., Microsoft Vista) have shifted the balance slightly.

UNIX Operating System

The UNIX OS was originally developed at Bell Labs in 1969. Today, UNIX is used to refer to a number of open-source operating systems that function according to UNIX specifications. UNIX-like systems do not completely meet these standards, but some of these, such as Linux, are also popular. UNIX pioneered many aspects of modern operating systems, including portability, networking, and even the eventual development of the Internet.

The most common use of the UNIX OS is in servers and workstations. Its processing power is much greater than that of Windows, and it is much more stable and has more extensive security features. The majority of the Internet works from UNIX-based servers.

Macintosh OS

The latest versions of the Macintosh OS are OS X 10.5, also called Leopard, and its upgrade Snow Leopard (OS X 10.6). While earlier Macintosh operating systems could run only on Macintosh-specific processors, Leopard supports both Macintosh and Intel processors, and Snow Leopard runs only on Intel processors. Apple computers have long been the computers of choice for those who work in graphics-heavy industries such as graphic design and layout. CGI work that is popular in today's movies is often performed on Apple machines. Video editing is also a Macintosh-centric industry. Major motion pictures such as Cold Mountain have been edited on Final Cut Pro, a Macintosh-specific editing program. Professional musicians also gravitate to Apple computers, using ProTools for tracking, mixing, and editing of music tracks.

Physical Systems and Virtual Systems

A company's physical systems consist of physical resources such as personnel, equipment, computers, and funds. A virtual system consists of information and data. The virtual system is usually used to represent the elements of the physical system. An example of a physical system would be a company's actual inventory of products stored in a warehouse. A virtual system would

Copyright © Mometrix Media. You have been licensed one copy of this document for personal use only. Any other reproduction or redistribution is strictly prohibited. All rights reserved.
This content is provided for test preparation purposes only and does not imply an endorsement by Mometrix of any particular political, scientific, or religious point of view.

be the electronic records of the existing inventory and the computer system used to manage and keep track of inventory as it changes through the course of doing business.

Open System Versus a Closed System

An open system is a system that interacts with the outside world. Physical or virtual resources flow back and forth between a company and its customers, producing an open system. In a closed system, there is no interaction with the outside world. In a typical company, both physical and virtual systems are open systems, as they must communicate with employees, customers, and other aspects of the surrounding environment in order for the company to be successful. Information systems users typically do not deal with closed systems, as they are of little use to a dynamic business.

Operating System

An operating system is the program in a computer that performs the basic tasks of maintaining the computer, running software, and producing the user interface. As computers developed, programmers realized that the majority of computer programs and functions required an identical or similar set of commands to support the operation of the computer itself, as well as the execution of multiple individual programs. As programming became more sophisticated, these common commands and functions were combined and eventually became known as the computer operating system.

Software for specific use cannot function on a computer without an operating system, and must be programmed to accommodate the basic needs of the computer's OS. For example, software programmed for a Windows OS will not operate on a Macintosh OS, unless the programmer has made allowances for both operating systems.

User-Friendly Software

User-friendly software is software that is easy for a user to understand and use. Typically, user-friendly software requires less training to use, with functionality that is intuitive to the user.

Five major characteristics of user-friendly software are:

- Easily accessible menus, drop-downs and icons that often accomplish the same task, giving users execution options to fit their preferences and skill levels
- A graphical interface with graphics that are easily understood and standardized
- Help provided directly by the software when requested
- Forms and templates to be used for basic functions
- Information within the program that indicates what input the program requires

Data and Information

Information is a term used to refer to data that has been processed so that it is easily understandable and usable. Data consists of all the raw numbers, facts, and statistics generated by a company or program. When this data is processed into a usable, understandable form such as a graph or chart, it becomes information.

One major example of data becoming information is accounting data. Without organization and context, accounting data is meaningless. Once it has been organized into a meaningful format, it becomes useful information. Since this is a large, labor-intensive job, it is not surprising that one of the first uses of computers was in processing accounting, billing, inventory, and other similar data.

Copyright © Mometrix Media. You have been licensed one copy of this document for personal use only. Any other reproduction or redistribution is strictly prohibited. All rights reserved.
This content is provided for test preparation purposes only and does not imply an endorsement by Mometrix of any particular political, scientific, or religious point of view.

Transaction Processing System

Early computer systems were referred to as electronic data processing systems. Since pre-computer electronic systems were largely used to process data into a more usable form, early computers also focused on this task. A later term, "accounting information systems," grew from the prevalence of computer use to handle accounting data.

Transaction processing system is used more commonly today to refer to what a computing system does. A transaction processing system receives data as input, then performs transactions on that data in order to process it and change it into a form that is usable and easily understood by individual employees and managers who must use the data for decision making and record keeping.

MIS

A management information system (MIS) uses computers to process data, make it usable and available to users in a company. These users typically need similar information to be made available in various formats.

MIS makes use of report-writing software that produces reports according to a set schedule. These reports can be produced regularly or as ad-hoc reports, which are special reports generated for a specific need that does not require a regular schedule. MIS also uses mathematical models based on a company's standard operations. These models are generated from existing data about the company and can be used to make predictions about the company's future or to produce simulations to determine the feasibility of specific programs or decisions.

IOS

An interorganizational information system, or IOS, involves not only a company, but also that company's customers, suppliers, and other elements of the infrastructure. The management information system provides information that can be disseminated throughout an IOS, so that this important information is supplied to everyone who needs access to it. An IOS greatly reduces the effort needed to send information to everyone within an organization and to those outside the main organization who need it in the course of doing everyday business.

Virtual Office System

A virtual office system functions based on office automation techniques that allow communication to occur throughout an office or company via electronic means. Examples include email, teleconferencing, voice-mail systems, and faxes. The majority of computer and computer application use in most modern companies involves communications technology that allows the production of a virtual office system.

With virtual office systems, not only the local office is able to communicate more efficiently. Virtual office systems also allow easier real-time communication with personnel in satellite offices or subsidiaries in other countries.

GUI

Graphical user interface, or GUI, refers to the use of graphics and icons to provide a visual representation of a computer's functionality. Instead of using text commands in a command line, users can simply choose a graphic or icon and activate an action or program by activating that icon.

While text-based or command-line systems require alphanumeric keyboard input, GUIs typically work through point-and-click functions using a mouse or similar device such as a touch pad on a laptop. GUIs are overall very user-friendly and popular among computer users.

Copyright © Mometrix Media. You have been licensed one copy of this document for personal use only. Any other reproduction or redistribution is strictly prohibited. All rights reserved.
This content is provided for test preparation purposes only and does not imply an endorsement by Mometrix of any particular political, scientific, or religious point of view.

Two Basic Types of Software

The two basic types of software are system software and application software.

System software, or operating system software, allows the computer to quickly and easily perform basic tasks common to most users and applications. It functions as the computer's basic "brain," handling connections between hardware and software, and powering the user interface, input, and output.

Application software allows the computer to perform specialized functionality, from data processing to graphics manipulation to gaming. Application software cannot function without system software, but provides the user with additional tools designed to perform specific actions and tasks.

Application Software Categories

There are three major categories of application software, based on where and how they are produced:

- *Prewritten software:* The majority of software used by individuals and companies is prewritten or off-the-shelf software. This includes programs such as Microsoft Office, Photoshop, Outlook, and various Internet browsers. Prewritten software is generally easy to obtain and affordable.
- *Custom software*: Custom application software is written specifically to a company's needs. A company might outsource software development to another company or maintain a dedicated staff to produce custom software.
- *User-written software*: Users sometimes write their own applications to meet individual needs. Various prewritten software packages include functionality that allows users to assemble small programs within the software to handle common tasks.

Personal Productivity Systems

Personal productivity systems are vital to virtual networks. These software systems typically automate general clerical tasks such as accounting, word processing, and other types of data organization. The Microsoft Office Suite is an example of a personal productivity system.

Personal productivity systems can also be used to maintain contact lists, calendars, and other information important to office management. Email clients are also personal productivity systems. The prevalence of email in the modern office has greatly increased productivity and virtually eliminated the traditional memorandum. Email also allows instantaneous communication throughout an organization, even when branches are located in different states or countries.

Copyright © Mometrix Media. You have been licensed one copy of this document for personal use only. Any other reproduction or redistribution is strictly prohibited. All rights reserved.
This content is provided for test preparation purposes only and does not imply an endorsement by Mometrix of any particular political, scientific, or religious point of view.

Telecommunications and Networks

Modem

A modem, or modulator-demodulator, was originally used to modulate existing analog telephone signals to carry digital data, then demodulate the digital data to decode it. These devices were used to transmit digital information from computers over standard telephone lines, which were not constructed for this function.

The need for new ways to transmit digital data began to grow as more people began to make use of Internet services, leading to new types of modems. The telephone modem is still in use in some areas, but faster devices have become more common. For example, the cable modem uses the cable provided for cable television service to transmit digital signals.

ISDN and DSL

Integrated Services Digital Network (ISDN) and Digital Subscriber Line (DSL) connections are also ways to transmit digital information over phone lines, but they work differently from the traditional telephone modem.

ISDN and DSL use digital protocols rather than analog signals. When the demand for Internet use began to burgeon, telephone companies responded by adding digital protocols to formerly analog telephone lines. Digital information is transmitted in packets, dividing the digital information into various pieces that each hold information about the transmitting and receiving computers. Packets are transmitted separately, then collected at the destination and reassembled in order.

VPN

VPN stands for virtual private network. Many corporations make use of VPNs to take advantage of the security of a private connection combined with the speed and convenience of an Internet connection. A VPN requires use of tunneling software that is used to set up the path the data will take through existing equipment.

VPNs can save companies a great deal of money compared to using a dedicated line for information transmission. It also provides a higher level of security than using public Internet connections to communicate between company machines, and so represents an affordable compromise between the two approaches.

TCP/IP

TCP/IP stands for Transmission Control Protocol/Internet Protocol. TCP/IP is a widely used type of packet-switching protocol. TCP/IP handles data being transmitted between individual computers, and is used in most personal computers to manage Internet connections. The TCP part of the protocol manages the communication over the network. The IP part handles individual packets, routing them from computer to computer. The IP protocol makes use of an individual computer's IP address to properly route packets to their destination. The IP address uses a series of numbers to identify the network as well as the host, the sub-network, and the individual computer.

VoIP

Another digital protocol, VoIP, stands for Voice over Internet Protocol. This protocol allows voice data to be transmitted over Internet lines. Some phone services now use VoIP instead of traditional phone lines.

Copyright © Mometrix Media. You have been licensed one copy of this document for personal use only. Any other reproduction or redistribution is strictly prohibited. All rights reserved.
This content is provided for test preparation purposes only and does not imply an endorsement by Mometrix of any particular political, scientific, or religious point of view.

Networks

A network is any group of computers connected together. It can also include devices such as printers and scanners. There are several types of networks, defined based on their overall size and the type of users they connect.

LAN

Local Area Network: A LAN is the smallest type of network, limited to about a half a mile total. Individual elements are generally no more than 60 feet apart. LANs operate over private networks.

MAN

Metropolitan Area Network: This kind of network can cover a distance of up to 30 miles. A MAN is often used to connect different buildings in a single complex, such as within a large corporation or a university campus. MANs also work over private networks.

WAN

Wide Area Network: A WAN connects large areas using public telephone systems. WANs have been largely displaced by Internet connections.

Internet, Intranet, and Extranet

The Internet refers to the worldwide series of interconnected networks that allows computers to connect to each other all over the world. The Internet as an entity is publicly accessible.

An intranet is a smaller network that uses the same protocols as the Internet but is restricted, usually to a specific company or a small group of people within a company or organization. It differs from a LAN in that it can connect to other networks, but is blocked from them through the use of firewalls or other security measures.

An extranet is created when an intranet must be expanded to accommodate a limited number of outside users. The connection is usually established through the Internet, and kept secure via firewalls.

Peer-to-peer Protocol

Early computers only had to communicate with a display terminal. As machines became more sophisticated, however, technology had to be developed to allow greater communication. Companies began to define peer-to-peer protocols to determine how this communication would be handled.

System Network Architecture, or SNA, was an early protocol that allowed a host computer to communicate with other computers by polling them in sequence.

The Token Ring protocol followed SNA and did not require a host machine. Each computer could act as a controller, passing a virtual control "token" from computer to computer.

The Ethernet protocol was developed in the 1970s and is still in use today. Ethernet is known as an open protocol. Any computer can send information at any time. If data is sent simultaneously by more than one computer, a data-transmission crash occurs, and the data is resent.

Networks and Telecommunications Importance

One of the most powerful uses for company networks is the sharing of information. Data can be transmitted between individuals and groups almost instantaneously, allowing efficient teamwork

Copyright © Mometrix Media. You have been licensed one copy of this document for personal use only. Any other reproduction or redistribution is strictly prohibited. All rights reserved.
This content is provided for test preparation purposes only and does not imply an endorsement by Mometrix of any particular political, scientific, or religious point of view.

among groups in different areas of the company. Telecommunications and company networks often allow different groups to work together from different areas of the country or even worldwide.

On a smaller scale, company networks allow data to be collected in one place from a variety of networked machines, reducing the labor involved in gathering information from individual employees. Various company records such as real-time inventory, employee availability, individual outlet performance for retail stores, and other important data can be accessed from any machine connected to the network.

Personal Productivity Systems

Personal productivity systems are vital to virtual networks. These software systems typically automate general clerical tasks such as accounting, word processing, and other types of data organization. The Microsoft Office Suite is an example of a personal productivity system.

Personal productivity systems can also be used to maintain contact lists, calendars, and other information important to office management. Email clients are also personal productivity systems. The prevalence of email in the modern office has greatly increased productivity and virtually eliminated the traditional memorandum. Email also allows instantaneous communication throughout an organization, even when branches are located in different states or countries.

Email Uses

The use of email in the corporate setting has eliminated the traditional hard-copy memorandum. It has also increased communication speed and enabled more direct contact between employees and management or between different company divisions and organizations.

Through networking, employees not only can communicate with each other more efficiently, but also can coordinate schedules using online, networked calendars and scheduling software. An entire department can coordinate its schedules through a networked calendar, making it simple for any single member of the organization to find another person's availability to plan meetings or travel.

Internet, Instant Messaging, and Blogs

The Internet allows numerous tasks to be completed from a single location. Companies can order supplies, pay bills, or research other companies' activities using a simple web browser. Doing business through the Internet also provides the possibility of e-commerce—selling products directly to consumers through an online storefront.

Instant messaging (IM), while often looked down on in a corporate setting, can provide instantaneous communication between employees and even a simple way to set up meetings among groups through use of IM chat rooms. Unlike email, IM communication occurs in real time, and several people can discuss an issue at once.

A corporation can use a blog to post news and information about the company. The information can help prospective customers find the company and learn about the company's products and policies. The blog can also provide information to employees and present a corporate "face" to create a more personal relationship with customers.

Groupware

Groupware is a type of software that allows more than one person to work on a single document. The document itself remains in a central location, accessible by individuals on a network. When one

Copyright © Mometrix Media. You have been licensed one copy of this document for personal use only. Any other reproduction or redistribution is strictly prohibited. All rights reserved.
This content is provided for test preparation purposes only and does not imply an endorsement by Mometrix of any particular political, scientific, or religious point of view.

individual makes a change, that change is highlighted so others working on the same document will be able to see it clearly.

Groupware can allow groups to share scheduling and calendar information, work on editing corporate documents, reports, or spreadsheets, or collaborate on any other type of work, all from different locations. Online tools such as Google Documents and Google Calendars can perform a function similar to that of groupware.

TELECOMMUTING

Telecommuting allows employees to work from a remote location, usually from home, either full time or on specified days. Telecommuting can require special access to the company's computers from a remote work location via a VPN or other arrangement. In other cases, telecommuters work from local offices connected to the main office via the Internet.

It is estimated that as much as a quarter of today's work force telecommutes at least part of the time. Studies also show that telecommuting workers are actually up to 15 percent more productive. Some companies use special software to track worker productivity while they are telecommuting. Others employ tools that help increase the efficiency of collaborative work across locations.

TELECOMMUNICATIONS SYSTEMS AND INTERNATIONAL BUSINESS

With an efficient telecommunications system, a company can conduct international business efficiently and without the extreme overhead traditionally associated with international enterprise. Electronic communication can provide immediate access to a customer's needs or inventory. Orders can arrive instantaneously via email rather than having to be delayed by transport through the mail. Even monetary conversion is simplified, with real-time exchange rates available at a moment's notice.

Using the advantages telecommunications provides, even small businesses can pursue international business dealings without having to spend prohibitive amounts of money for everyday communication, and large businesses can greatly streamline their international operations.

NETWORKING AND TELECOMMUNICATIONS

Making use of networking and telecommunications in a business can provide a wide variety of tools for individual employees that might not otherwise be available. Persons with disabilities can make use of company-wide tools for communication and other means of simplifying their jobs and making it possible for them to do work they would not otherwise be able to do. Individual schedules can be more flexible through the use of telecommuting that allows employees to work from home during family emergencies or weather complications. In cases where the job demands, telecommunications networks allow employees to be available for emergencies when they are away from the office, often without having to leave home, thus creating less disruption in their individual schedules.

SERVERS AND CLIENTS

A server in a computer network is a centralized computer that holds data. Other computers on the network can retrieve data from or save data to the server. Servers come in a wide range of sizes, from an ordinary PC chosen to function as a server to larger computers specifically designed to work efficiently and smoothly with all the computers on the network. Often a network server is used to provide accessibility to certain data across the network and backup storage space for the entire network. It is important to consider scalability when choosing a server. Scalability refers to the ability to enlarge server speed, space, and performance as the company grows.

Copyright © Mometrix Media. You have been licensed one copy of this document for personal use only. Any other reproduction or redistribution is strictly prohibited. All rights reserved.
This content is provided for test preparation purposes only and does not imply an endorsement by Mometrix of any particular political, scientific, or religious point of view.

A client computer is a computer that is attached to the network and is typically used by an individual. The client computer can retrieve data from the server and also save data to it. A client computer is sometimes referred to as a workstation.

Server Farm Construction

A server farm refers to a group of servers connected to each other. Using integration technology, these servers can communicate with each other to function as a single large server. Storage and processing are distributed across the collection of servers. Server farms provide scalability because additional servers can be added to the connection to provide additional space and processing power. Some companies use hundreds or even thousands of smaller servers integrated to form one large farm.

Peer-to-Peer Networking and Grid Computing

In peer-to-peer networking, single computers within the system are used as both servers and clients. The network can work with a single computer working as a server or with several computers in the network taking on this role as well as functioning as individual employee workstations. Grid computing works in a similar way, allowing processing and storage to be broken up among numerous computers within a single organization. Software designed specifically for this function allows the computers to share the computing needs.

SAN, NIC, and LAN Cards

SAN refers to storage area network. A SAN allows multiple storage devices to be connected to a single computer. These storage devices can be on or off the main network. Devices usually include external hard drives. Separating the storage from the internal storage in the computer protects data in case of malfunctions in the main computer and lends it portability.

NIC is a network interface card, also referred to as a LAN (local area network) card. The card is installed in an individual computer and allows the computer to communicate with other computers across the network, including any server, servers, or additional storage devices that are also on the network.

Hub, Switch, and Router

Hubs, switches, and routers are devices that allow smaller networks to be joined together to form larger networks. They are often confused, but they function differently.

Hub: A hub is a simple connection device that allows several computers or devices to communicate with each other through the hub. It does not analyze or direct the data that comes through it.

Router: A router analyzes packets as they pass through it and determines where they should be sent. By properly directing packets of data, a router can greatly increase the efficiency of a network.

Switch: Like a router, a switch analyzes data packets. When transmitting data, however, a switch isolates a single line, causing it to be dedicated to that transmission for a period of time. More advanced routers function as both routers and switches.

Copyright © Mometrix Media. You have been licensed one copy of this document for personal use only. Any other reproduction or redistribution is strictly prohibited. All rights reserved.
This content is provided for test preparation purposes only and does not imply an endorsement by Mometrix of any particular political, scientific, or religious point of view.

Network Types

Different types of networks perform slightly different functions. Functional networks often combine elements of each of the three main types.

- *Shared-media networks*: A shared-media network makes use of a single connection. Protocols such as Ethernet determine which machine is allowed to communicate at any one time
- *Switched networks*: These networks make use of switches, with one attached to each networked computer. The switch determines where individual packets of data should be directed. Switched networks tend to be faster than shared-media networks
- *Enterprise networks*: An enterprise network connects numerous sub-networks across an entire company. Enterprise networks require numerous protocols, wide area networks (WANs), and other hardware and software arrangements to work efficiently

Network Security

Due to the nature of business, companies share a great deal of proprietary information over networks. This information must be protected. Network security protects data in several ways, including:

- Protecting outside networks from accessing the internal network
- Preventing internal network users from accessing dangerous external sites
- Preventing viruses and other malicious software from infecting the network
- Network security can function at several levels, from mechanisms to protect the entire network to software to protect individual workstations

Company Security Policy Implementation

The five phases of implementing a company security policy are:

- *Project initiation*—in this phase, an MIS committee or other group is chosen to steer the project
- *Policy development*—the steering team consults with various individuals throughout the company to develop security policies
- *Consultation and approval*—proposals and findings are brought to management for approval
- *Awareness and education*—training begins in various departments to initiate implementation of the policy
- *Policy dissemination*—security policies are enacted throughout the company, typically via meetings with employees to explain policies and procedures

A Control

A control is a way to reduce risks to a company or prevent risks from occurring. The three categories of controls are technical, formal, and informal controls.

- *Technical controls*: These types of controls are built into systems from the beginning. Technical controls include access controls, intrusion-detection systems, firewalls and cryptography, and physical controls such as simply locking the door to the computer room
- *Formal controls*: These refer to policies and procedures, codes of conduct, and overall monitoring of the system. These controls allow the company to act when policies are not followed

Copyright © Mometrix Media. You have been licensed one copy of this document for personal use only. Any other reproduction or redistribution is strictly prohibited. All rights reserved.
This content is provided for test preparation purposes only and does not imply an endorsement by Mometrix of any particular political, scientific, or religious point of view.

- *Informal controls*: In order to understand policies and procedures, employees must be exposed to them and trained in what is expected of them. This kind of training is an informal control

Access Controls

Access controls determine who can gain access to the network or portions of the network. The three steps of access control determine who is trying to access the network and whether they should be allowed to do so. The three steps of access control are:

- User identification—the user enters a user name and password to identify himself
- User authentication—requires a physical item such as an access card for further identification
- User authorization—once the user has been identified and authenticated, he is allowed access to the network or parts of the network

The first two steps make use of user profiles that describe authorized users. The authorization step uses access-control files that tell what parts of the network each user is allowed to access.

Types of Intrusion Detection

Intrusion detection identifies an unauthorized entry into the system and stops the attempt before it can cause harm to the system. The best-known form of intrusion detection is virus-protection software. Virus protection is largely aimed at preventing viruses from entering the system via email or through Internet browsing.

Insider-threat prediction evaluates a user's identification to determine whether he might be a threat. These prediction tools will evaluate the user's position, default access, and other elements of his user profile to determine whether he is a threat.

Firewall Function

A firewall provides a protective barrier between a company network and outside networks such as the Internet in general. The firewall is software that is intended to protect the entire network rather than individual computers. The firewall can be set up to filter certain domains, certain IP addresses, or specific file types from crossing into or accessing the network. The level of protection is determined by how the firewall itself is configured.

Firewall software is available for use on individual computers as well, through the operating system itself or from popular virus-protection software companies such as Norton and McAfee.

Three Types of Firewalls

There are three basic types of firewalls.

- *Packet-filtering firewall*: This type of firewall uses a router. The router uses programmed tables of IP addresses that indicate what data should be allowed through and what should be blocked
- *Circuit-level firewall*: This type of firewall is closer to the circuit than a router is. This allows for a higher level of filtering as well as a safer overall system
- *Application-level firewall*: This requires specific information such as a user name, password, or other authentication to be entered directly into an application. This allows for an even higher level of security, but it depends on a particular application being available and properly programmed to authenticate users

Copyright © Mometrix Media. You have been licensed one copy of this document for personal use only. Any other reproduction or redistribution is strictly prohibited. All rights reserved.
This content is provided for test preparation purposes only and does not imply an endorsement by Mometrix of any particular political, scientific, or religious point of view.

Most companies use a combination of all these types of firewalls for the most efficient protection.

Cryptography

Cryptography uses mathematical formulas to encrypt data as it is transmitted over the network. Even if the data is intercepted, it cannot be interpreted without decryption.

Cryptography is widely used in e-commerce applications to protect personal information such as credit card data, addresses, and Social Security numbers. Secure Electronic Transaction (SET) is one cryptography protocol that uses digital signatures to identify legitimate customers or merchants and to protect information stored in banks and other financial institutions. Certain restrictions exist regarding cryptography due to concerns by the government that encrypted communication could be used for terrorism or other illegal activity.

Protocol

A protocol is a set of rules and definitions that determines how the different pieces of a network communicate with each other. These rules help the system avoid various problems that could slow or halt communications.

Protocols can be enacted by software or hardware or both. The simplest protocols determine how pieces of hardware interact. More complex protocols deal with all the intricacies of electronic communication, including dealing with corrupt or incomplete data, ensuring email arrives at the correct destination, and even interpreting websites correctly through the HTTP protocol. Protocols underlie all the basic functionality of electronic communications.

Main Functions of a Protocol

A protocol performs four basic functions:

- Provides a way to refer to each individual user on the system
- Provides rules to determine which user is allowed to communicate at any given time
- Determines duration of communication for individual senders
- Determines what to do if two or more users or computers attempt to communicate simultaneously

By resolving these basic issues, protocols facilitate efficient communication over a networked system.

CSMA/CD Protocol

CSMA/CD stands for Carrier Sense Multiple Access with Collision Detection. This protocol is also known as the Ethernet protocol, and is widely used in communications networks. The Ethernet protocol allows any LAN card on the network to transmit after it checks to see if another card is transmitting. This is the carrier-sense part of the protocol. After the line clears, the LAN card may transmit. The protocol then limits the amount of time it may transmit to keep that transmission from blocking the available lines. Ethernet works best with high-speed connections, because the higher speed reduces the number of collisions. With many users on a single system and a slower connection, collisions become frequent and can severely bog down the system.

Security Topology

Security topology involves the way the physical components of a network are configured. The topology of a network is based on different levels of access required by different individuals on the network. For example, if a company has an e-commerce site, certain servers will have to be set up

Copyright © Mometrix Media. You have been licensed one copy of this document for personal use only. Any other reproduction or redistribution is strictly prohibited. All rights reserved.
This content is provided for test preparation purposes only and does not imply an endorsement by Mometrix of any particular political, scientific, or religious point of view.

so that customers can access data stored on them. Other data, such as sensitive company information, will have to be stored on secure servers. A company might also need to have an intranet, accessible only by persons within the company, and an extranet that is accessible only by certain individuals or locations outside the company. These various needs are taken into consideration to determine appropriate security topologies.

Network Infrastructure Construction

The infrastructure of the network not only provides the equipment to run the network, but also determines the network's speed and potential for easy expansion. An infrastructure should support existing needs, but should also leave room for upgrades, increased storage, increased speed, and other changes that will be required as the company grows and technology changes. Security should also take these considerations into account as corporate needs grow and change. Set-ups like server farms, where additional servers can be easily added, help to produce a flexible infrastructure.

Redundancy on a Network

Redundancy means that several portions of a network can perform the same job. For example, if one server becomes inoperable, another server or servers can step in to take over the workload without interruption to business functions. Redundancy is also important to security functions, so that if one part of the system fails to neutralize a threat, another part will be able to intercept it.

Building redundancy into a network helps prevent downtime or complete shutdowns of the system. The more important the functions performed on a network, the more important redundancy becomes. An efficient network topology will take redundancy into account, and ensure that sufficient backup exists for all processes taking place on the system.

Copyright © Mometrix Media. You have been licensed one copy of this document for personal use only. Any other reproduction or redistribution is strictly prohibited. All rights reserved.
This content is provided for test preparation purposes only and does not imply an endorsement by Mometrix of any particular political, scientific, or religious point of view.

Business Information Systems

E-COMMERCE

E-commerce can be both narrowly and broadly defined. The narrowest definition is limited to interaction with customers and product suppliers through the Internet. The broader definition involves these interactions as well as any business interactions that occur within the firm. E-commerce, then, represents any function within the company that makes use of a computer that is on the network and uses a web browser. This can include operations in any department within the company, from actual sales of products to customers to functions within the finance department or human resources.

B2C AND B2B E-COMMERCE

B2C, or business-to-consumer e-commerce, refers to direct sales of goods to the company's customers. B2C requires an extensive infrastructure that guarantees ease of use by customers in order for them to navigate the company's e-commerce website to make purchases. Transactions are usually small, but can range from a single item purchased to a large quantity. B2B, or business-to-business e-commerce, involves interaction between businesses. In these cases, neither business is the actual consumer. These could involve transactions between the company and a supplier, or between a manufacturer and a retailer, for example. B2B e-commerce involves a much smaller, more specialized group of people, but the transactions can involve large quantities of goods and large sums of money.

BENEFITS AND CONSTRAINTS OF E-COMMERCE

Several benefits can be expected when a company institutes e-commerce:

- Better customer service
- Better relationships with suppliers
- Better relationships with financial entities
- Better return on investment
- Integrating e-commerce into a company usually results in improved function across the board, including higher profits

Common constraints that prevent companies from pursuing e-commerce include:

- Cost
- Security
- Software availability

The cost of e-commerce continues to drop along with most other technology-related items. Security issues have also been addressed more thoroughly in recent years, and software continues to become less expensive and more readily available, reducing these concerns for even the smallest companies.

E-COMMERCE AND HOW IT IS CHANGING

The actual scope of e-commerce is constantly changing as technology advances and becomes less expensive. The growth rate in e-commerce remains consistently high, though the majority continues to focus on B2B rather than B2C. However, more and more direct customer sales occur through e-commerce every year. Retailers have come to depend more and more on their online presence to affect sales. Even during the holidays, traditionally an active period, more consumers

Copyright © Mometrix Media. You have been licensed one copy of this document for personal use only. Any other reproduction or redistribution is strictly prohibited. All rights reserved.
This content is provided for test preparation purposes only and does not imply an endorsement by Mometrix of any particular political, scientific, or religious point of view.

have turned to online shopping. Companies that have depended on physical outlets have focused additional resources on online storefronts, enabling the consumer to purchase goods through either method. This flexibility allows customers to shop the way they choose, and provides additional outlets for businesses to sell their products.

IMPLEMENTING E-COMMERCE

Implementing e-commerce in a company can be an extensive and costly endeavor. A company should evaluate the benefits versus the drawbacks to ensure that e-commerce will be profitable in the long run. In order to establish a strategic plan to implement e-commerce, the company acquires business intelligence by gathering data about the firm and all the various environmental elements with which the firm interacts. This business intelligence can be gathered through two major sources: external databases and search engines. External databases provide information from a huge number of sources, including news sources and data about other businesses. Search engines can quickly and easily gather information from anywhere on the Internet that can then be compiled and used in the decision-making process. Once sufficient business information is gathered, the company can make the decision regarding implementing e-commerce.

IOS AND EDI

An interorganizational system (IOS) consists of several firms connected through electronic means. These firms then work together and are referred to as trading partners, a business alliance, or business partners. A vital part of an IOS is e-commerce that allows the firms to interact and share data.

EDI, or electronic data interchange, is part of an IOS. EDI functions as part of the infrastructure of the IOS, providing the means for the different firms to communicate with each other. However, in some cases, EDI and IOS are used interchangeably. Some organizations use extranets to communicate between firms rather than EDI, but the majority still makes use of EDI. One form of EDI is a value-added network (VAN), which provides additional services to manage and operate communications rather than just making communication possible. A VAN is typically managed by an outside vendor.

IOS BENEFITS

IOS leads to major benefits for all companies involved in the relationship. The two major benefits of IOS are comparative efficiency and bargaining power.

- Comparative efficiency means that all the firms in the IOS can work more efficiently, lowering costs and expenses. Internal efficiency increases, allowing the firms to operate more smoothly. Interorganizational efficiency also improves so that the firms, while working together, can provide more products for more customers
- Bargaining power is increased when firms work together to manage problems with suppliers or customers. Three basic areas contribute to bargaining power in an IOS:
    - Unique products and product features
    - Reduced costs related to searching for products and suppliers
    - Greater cost to the customer to change to another supplier

Another IOS, vendor stock replenishment, is established when a supplier is allowed access to a customer's inventory to provide automatic restocking.

Copyright © Mometrix Media. You have been licensed one copy of this document for personal use only. Any other reproduction or redistribution is strictly prohibited. All rights reserved.
This content is provided for test preparation purposes only and does not imply an endorsement by Mometrix of any particular political, scientific, or religious point of view.

SIX INDIRECT BENEFITS OF IOS

In addition to the direct benefits of IOS, six indirect benefits often also come about:

- Overall cost reduction
- Fewer data-entry errors
- Greater efficiency
- Stronger competitive advantage
- Better customer service
- Better relationships with partners

All of these benefits can lead to increased profits and other distinct advantages for the companies involved in the IOS.

B2C E-COMMERCE STRATEGIES

B2C e-commerce is growing rapidly, and companies are pursuing a variety of strategies to take advantage of the expanding market. Three major strategies for B2C e-commerce are:

- *Digital product sales*: An increasing number of products, including music, books, movies, and television shows, can be sold directly to the customer in digital format. A customer does not have to wait for products to be delivered, but can purchase, download, and use the products almost immediately
- *Physical product sales:* Physical products can be purchased over the Internet, but then must be shipped to the customer, adding to the company overhead. Online sales have largely supplanted traditional catalog sales, with customers placing their orders over the Internet rather than over the phone or by mail. This kind of virtual sale is also useful for smaller companies that cannot afford a storefront
- *Hybrid product sales:* In these cases, companies offer both an online and a physical store where products can be purchased

E-COMMERCE FUTURE

Several elements are contributing to rapid change and growth in e-commerce. One is the increase of mobile commerce, in which e-commerce is accomplished via mobile devices such as cell phones or personal digital assistants (PDAs). Mobile commerce is typically wireless and takes advantage of third-generation (3G) telecommunications systems. Mobile devices can now offer news, weather, banking, and financial services; easy, mobile access to the Internet for purchasing on the go; and limitless access to quick and easy communication; this limitless ability to communicate promises to bring even more growth to e-commerce.

DSS

A decision support system (DSS) assists managers and teams of employees in decision making. The DSS retrieves data, evaluates that data to produce models, and then provides a visual representation of the expected results. A manager or management team can use these models to make a final decision. An example might be a model forecasting future sales.

ERPs

Enterprise resource planning systems (ERPs) combine management information systems and decision support systems into a comprehensive package. These packages provide standardized software to help integrate management across an entire organization. ERP systems are quite expensive and so are typically used only by very large corporations.

Copyright © Mometrix Media. You have been licensed one copy of this document for personal use only. Any other reproduction or redistribution is strictly prohibited. All rights reserved.
This content is provided for test preparation purposes only and does not imply an endorsement by Mometrix of any particular political, scientific, or religious point of view.

AI

Artificial intelligence, or AI, is programming built into a computer that helps its behavior approach that of a human brain. In the case of decision support systems (DSS), the software makes use of a large amount of data related to a specific question or problem. The program analyzes this data and processes it in such as way as to represent the variety of outcomes a human decision maker or team of decision makers might expect from that data. It also can produce an idea of what the results of various decisions might be.

OLAP

OLAP, or online analytical processing, provides managers and decision makers with quick and easy access to data stored in a data warehouse. OLAP allows rapid response to complex queries, making data analysis and decision making more efficient.

EIS

The executive information system (EIS) is sometimes also referred to as an executive support system (ESS). The system provides upper management with high-level information on company performance. Workstations belonging to the managers access an executive database, where information has been processed by central computers. Information within the database can come from a variety of sources, including various staff members or external sources from which the database retrieves data on a regular basis. The exact type of information and how it is processed is determined by the manager in question. In some cases, a manager will prefer summary information, but other managers might prefer more detailed data. The MIS department will ensure the data provided to the executive database meets the needs of the particular executives who use it.

FIS

The financial information system (FIS) focuses specifically on the company's financial activities. Subsystems of the FIS might include:

- Internal audit
- Funds management
- Forecasting
- Control
- Financial intelligence
- Transaction processing

All of these subsystems work together to provide an integrated picture of the firm's overall financial activities and well-being; using these subsystems and output, such as economic trends forecasts, the overall movement of funds through the company, and company-wide control of finances, executives can accurately monitor the firm's financial health.

HRIS

The human resources information system (HRIS) maintains and processes information regarding the company's human resources activities. Subsystems within the HRIS include:

- Recruiting
- Work force management
- Work force planning
- Compensation
- Benefits
- Workplace environment reporting

Copyright © Mometrix Media. You have been licensed one copy of this document for personal use only. Any other reproduction or redistribution is strictly prohibited. All rights reserved.
This content is provided for test preparation purposes only and does not imply an endorsement by Mometrix of any particular political, scientific, or religious point of view.

Input typically includes transaction processing as well as resource and intelligence subsystems. Output subsystems manage issues such as employee compensation and benefits, and also produce reports required by government agencies and other external regulatory organizations.

Manufacturing Information System

The manufacturing information system provides information about the firm's manufacturing processes. This typically includes:

- Inventory
- Cost
- Production
- Quality

Output subsystems within the manufacturing information system produce reports regarding all these concerns. An industrial engineering input subsystem is also often included, which involves data derived from studies conducted by industrial engineers within the company. These studies are designed to examine the company's overall efficiency. Executives can view this data and determine if the efficiency is up to desired levels and what decisions must be made to improve manufacturing activities throughout the firm.

MKIS

The marketing information system (MKIS) focuses on marketing efforts in the company. Input subsystems include the standard set of transaction processing, marketing research, and marketing intelligence. Output subsystems address the marketing mix, or the four main issues marketing managers must focus on to ensure customers' needs are met and the company remains profitable. These four issues are:

- Product
- Place
- Promotion
- Price

An additional output subsystem, the integrated-mix subsystem, helps managers develop high-level marketing strategies by combining the four elements of the marketing mix.

XML Role

XML, or extensible markup language, allows ease and efficiency in communication between various computers and computer systems. XML provides a simple and consistent means of formatting data so that it can be understood by different machines that might be operating on different software platforms. Even though each individual machine might format its data slightly differently, XML makes it easily translatable across the entire network. Use of XML continues to evolve and improve as it becomes more widespread. One technology that uses XML is simple object access protocol (SOAP), which provides a standard approach to how computers make use of objects across the Internet or other networks.

ERP

ERP has become vital to large companies because of its ability to integrate data from across the entire firm. ERP provides executives and decision makers with integrated information from all of the company's individual business systems, including accounting, human resources, and overall company logistics. ERP systems work in conjunction with the company's database management

Copyright © Mometrix Media. You have been licensed one copy of this document for personal use only. Any other reproduction or redistribution is strictly prohibited. All rights reserved.
This content is provided for test preparation purposes only and does not imply an endorsement by Mometrix of any particular political, scientific, or religious point of view.

system (DBMS), so that all the data within the DBMS is accessible to the ERP system. Large international companies in particular benefit from ERP systems because they are specifically meant to handle the volume of information these companies must deal with.

Another issue that led to the prevalence of ERP systems in the 1990s was the rise of the Y2K problem. Companies that were afraid their computer systems would be unable to handle the date changes required by the year 2000 and beyond purchased commercial ERP systems to replace their existing systems.

Drawbacks of ERP

Because of the complexity and specialized nature of ERP systems, only a few vendors deal with this type of software. Major companies include SAP and Oracle. With a limited number of companies providing the systems, ERP becomes an expensive investment. ERP typically includes expenses for software, licensing, and ongoing expense for maintenance and personnel to run the system. Initial training and other elements will also increase expenses until the system is running smoothly.

In making the decision to implement ERP, a company must consider all these factors. Most ERP systems offer similar functionality, so evaluation should consider ease of use, how easy the system is to customize, and whether it can easily manage international business if the firm requires this functionality.

ERP Advantages for International Businesses

ERP can be particularly useful for businesses that operate internationally. In fact, most ERP systems are specifically geared to provide this functionality for large businesses. Some features that ERP offers to international businesses include:

- Provides interface and reports in multiple languages
- Manages international currency and conversion
- Incorporates financial rules for individual countries
- Incorporates tax rules for individual countries

These functions are quite complex and add to the expense of ERP systems. However, for a company that deals with subsidiaries in many countries, being able to automatically incorporate currency and local regulations is vital in areas such as employee compensation.

ERP in Accounting

ERP systems provide a great deal of flexibility in dealing with a company's accounting information. ERP helps maintain general ledger accounts and ensures these accounts meet standards for each country in which the company functions. It also provides different management levels with the ability to produce sub-ledgers and sub-accounts so they can track activity in their individual departments. Any individual department can produce a specialized report at any time and be assured that the reports are based on current data. ERP systems also provide asset management, cash management, and other treasury functions as well as audit trails and basic controls expected from any accounting system. They also often include EIS functionality to allow managers to view details at any level, from high-level overviews and summaries to lower-level detail.

ERP in Human Resources

Regardless of the size of a company, employee compensation and benefits can provide many challenges for the human resources department. If a company works in multiple states or countries, these challenges become even more complicated. ERP helps handle these issues by providing

Copyright © Mometrix Media. You have been licensed one copy of this document for personal use only. Any other reproduction or redistribution is strictly prohibited. All rights reserved.
This content is provided for test preparation purposes only and does not imply an endorsement by Mometrix of any particular political, scientific, or religious point of view.

extensive documentation as well as reports in standardized formats acceptable to regulatory organizations such as state and federal government. They can also provide assistance to other HR tasks like training, travel, recruitment, and overall planning within the organization. Many also provide functionality so that employees can view certain personal data over the Internet and thus keep track of their taxes, benefits, training offered by the company, and other important information.

CRM

Any company's most valuable resource is its customers. With the rapid increase in ways to interact with customers, these various points of contact become more difficult to manage. A customer, though, still expects the company to remember past interactions, whether they occurred at a physical store, via an online store, or through a wireless connection or a phone call. CRM helps integrate all customer contact systems so this information is easy to compile and access.

Items tracked through CRM include:

- Prior purchase tracking
- Customer feedback
- Purchase patterns
- Cross-selling—recommending other products based on purchase patterns

CRM must also ensure that, despite the amount of information collected about individual customers, that information remains private and secure.

Typical CRM Package

An ERP system usually includes a CRM package to provide CRM functionality to the user. CRM packages provide easy access to a wide range of customer data, including recent purchases or returns, problems the customer may have had with purchases, and various other aspects of the customer's interaction with the company. When a customer service representative contacts or is contacted by a customer, that representative will be able to access information regarding that customer's activity.

The customer then feels that the company is doing its best to help because he or she does not have to supply a great deal of information in order to solve a problem. Customer service becomes quicker and more efficient, and customers receive better service overall.

CRM Drawbacks

CRM does present some drawbacks. CRM provided by an ERP system will have access to all basic transactions and records, but other information must be provided by salespeople within the company. These groups of people must be properly trained to provide all necessary data in order for CRM to work efficiently.

In addition, some customers resent having to provide detailed personal information and will be annoyed or offended by some CRM functionality instead of seeing it as a way to improve customer service. These customers should be provided with another way to contact the company that they are more comfortable using. Often a traditional outlet or ordering by mail is more appropriate for these customers.

Self-Service Customer Benefits

Another benefit of sophisticated CRM is that the company can provide self-service portals for customers so that they can perform many customer service duties on their own. For those who

Copyright © Mometrix Media. You have been licensed one copy of this document for personal use only. Any other reproduction or redistribution is strictly prohibited. All rights reserved.
This content is provided for test preparation purposes only and does not imply an endorsement by Mometrix of any particular political, scientific, or religious point of view.

would prefer to log in to a website to track orders rather than having to wait on the phone, this is an ideal solution. Customers can log in to their account with the company and check on order status, make new orders, pay outstanding bills, and even contact salespeople and customer service personnel directly if necessary. Frequently asked questions (FAQ) can be answered on the site through a direct interface, allowing many customers to troubleshoot problems without having to contact anyone. This can provide help to customers at any time of day or night, any day of the week, and can be a great help to customers with non-standard schedules.

SCM

Supply chain management (SCM) developed out of the needs of companies using mass production. In these companies, it is important that supply and demand be adequately measured to prevent the company from having too few or too many mass-produced products on the market at any given time. It is also important to monitor every aspect of the supply chain to ensure costs are as low as possible and profits are kept high. SCM can be seen as the flip side of ERP, focusing on a company's production departments rather than on administrative areas. SCM integrates these elements to increase efficiency, production and profit.

SCM BENEFITS

SCM integrates the overall supply chain starting at the very beginning of the chain—the customers. Mass production can focus more exactly on what customers need and want. A company can provide its exact needs to the supplier on an efficient timetable in order to meet manufacturing needs. Manufacturing is then monitored to ensure appropriate timelines and organization. Automation allows rapid, less expensive production and automated shipments to customers. With an integrated supply chain management system, a company can use mass customization to provide customers with exactly what they need. This technique produces customized products, but uses mass-production techniques, keeping prices lower.

SCM CHALLENGES

As with many powerful integration systems, SCM provides some challenges in its implementation. The major challenges to SCM are cost and acquiring the necessary relationships with outside firms along the supply chain. A smaller company might not be able to afford the complex integration required for efficient SCM. It also requires complex and sometimes costly electronic communication with suppliers all along the chain. The more automated the process is, the more efficient it will be, so these connections are vital to the most effective use of SCM. These connections require not only technology and various employees to manage SCM, but also a personal relationship with the companies in question that will allow freedom of access to various systems in both the supply chain companies and the main firm.

Copyright © Mometrix Media. You have been licensed one copy of this document for personal use only. Any other reproduction or redistribution is strictly prohibited. All rights reserved.
This content is provided for test preparation purposes only and does not imply an endorsement by Mometrix of any particular political, scientific, or religious point of view.

Systems Analysis and Design

SYSTEMS APPROACH TO PROBLEM SOLVING

The systems approach to problem solving involves a series of steps with defined goals.

- The first set of steps involves recognizing, defining, and understanding the problem
- The second step presents a variety of possible solutions to the problem
- The third step makes a choice among the possible solutions based on which solution will provide the best results

This form of problem solving is common in businesses today because it presents a blueprint that can be used to manage any business problems in an efficient manner that will produce a usable solution.

SYSTEMATIC PROBLEM SOLVING HISTORY

John Dewey, who was an early-twentieth-century professor of philosophy at Columbia University, can be credited with the origin of systematic problem solving. In 1910, he discussed three steps to resolving a controversy, which were to first recognize the controversy, then collect and evaluate various claims, and then make a final judgment or decision based on those claims. Although he did not refer to it as a systems approach, these ideas formed the groundwork for later application of systematic problem solving. This approach became popular in the 1960s and 1970s, when management scientists and information specialists developed the ideas into what is now known as the systems approach.

THREE PHASES OF THE SYSTEMS APPROACH

The systems approach to problem solving can be broken into three major phases:

- *Preparation effort:* This phase involves defining a business or company as a system or series of systems
- *Definition effort:* During this phase, a problem is defined and analyzed in detail at the subsystem level
- *Solution effort:* This phase focuses on finding a variety of solutions, evaluating them, selecting the best solution, and then putting it into play and ensuring its long-term effectiveness

PREPARATION EFFORT

The preparation effort involves three major steps. These steps can be pursued in any order, and do not have to fit within a specific time frame. In fact, these steps can begin to occur well before a specific problem must be addressed.

- In order to use the systems approach, the entire firm or company must be seen as a single system that adheres to a general systems model
- The firm must be seen as a system within its environment, including the ways in which it interacts with its environment
- The firm or company contains many subsystems—these must be identified. Some subsystems common to many companies include business areas, levels of management, and resource flows

The preparation effort can be, and often is, an ongoing process.

Copyright © Mometrix Media. You have been licensed one copy of this document for personal use only. Any other reproduction or redistribution is strictly prohibited. All rights reserved.
This content is provided for test preparation purposes only and does not imply an endorsement by Mometrix of any particular political, scientific, or religious point of view.

Definition Effort

The definition effort usually begins when a problem, symptom, or problem trigger becomes apparent. A problem trigger is a signal that an underlying condition could be overly harmful or unexpectedly beneficial to the company. A symptom is caused by the underlying problem, but often does not make the root problem immediately apparent. The problem itself is the specific occurrence or condition that is causing the problem trigger and the symptom. This could be a beneficial change or a harmful change. If it is a harmful change, the definition effort will focus on how to bring performance back on track. If it is a beneficial change, the definition effort will focus on how to sustain this change.

In order to complete the definition effort, the systems within the firm are analyzed, moving from systems level into subsystems. Individual system parts are also analyzed in a specific order.

Analyze Individual System Parts

There are seven individual steps to analyzing system parts during the definition effort. These steps must be pursued in order from first to last:

- *Evaluate existing standards*: These are usually set by management, along with the means of accurately measuring them. The system's results with the established standards. This evaluates the output of the system. If it is achieving the standards that have been established, the system is working well and this individual system does not require changes
- *Evaluate the system's management and organization*: This addresses both the personnel managing the system as well as the way the system's organization is structured
- *Evaluate the existing information system*: If the management team is sufficient, the information being sent to the system might not be
- Evaluate inputs as well as input resources. This addresses physical resources and how they flow through the system
- *Evaluate the system that changes input to output*: Input might be sufficient, but the process for transforming it might fall short
- *Evaluate output*: This addresses output resources such as shipping personnel, delivery fleet, and other items that deliver the system output to the final destination

Solution Effort

The definition effort, with its seven detailed steps, should pinpoint where the problem exists within the overall system structure. Once the problem has been identified and defined, the next step is to develop a solution. The five main steps of the solution effort are:

- Finding alternative solutions. For any given problem, there are always several possible solutions. This step identifies a variety of possibilities that could solve the problem
- Evaluate alternative solutions. The proposed solutions are measured against evaluation criteria to determine how well each solution would solve the problem
- Select the solution that will best solve the problem
- Implement that solution
- Ensure effectiveness of the solution

Copyright © Mometrix Media. You have been licensed one copy of this document for personal use only. Any other reproduction or redistribution is strictly prohibited. All rights reserved.
This content is provided for test preparation purposes only and does not imply an endorsement by Mometrix of any particular political, scientific, or religious point of view.

There are three ways to select the best solution among a list of many. These decision-making processes were identified by management theorist Henry Mintzberg:

- *Analysis:* Analysis involves evaluating the options in detail by presenting possible advantages and disadvantages as well as the overall effect of each solution on the entire firm. Analysis usually involves several levels of management or other teams formulating evaluations and presenting them to decision makers
- *Judgment*: This usually involves a single manager choosing the best solution based on his or her past experience
- *Bargaining:* This usually involves several managers negotiating among solutions to agree on one that will benefit all groups

MIS Steering Committee Role

A steering committee is a group of people who are brought together on a long-term but not necessarily permanent basis to provide direction, guidance, and control over a specific project. The MIS steering committee controls computer resource use within the firm. This group usually consists of several higher-level executives as well as lower-level managers and temporary consultants. The three main functions of the MIS steering committee are:

- *To establish policies*: These policies are based on ensuring necessary computer support for the firm's overall goals
- *Fiscal control:* The steering committee must approve any requests involving funds for computers and information resources within the firm
- *Conflict resolution*: The MIS steering committee will deal with any conflicts between groups regarding the use of computer resources

Decisions made by the MIS steering committee are based on executive strategies involving both the entire firm and MIS resources in general. Computer resources typically become more readily available, with better planning and control, under the guidance of the steering committee.

Purpose and Role of Project Management

Project management breaks a project down into steps, determines when those steps must occur, how long they will take, and what personnel must be available to implement them. Project management helps organize project teams for specific projects and assigns project leaders to direct the project. These teams are typically short-lived and move on to other projects upon project completion.

Tools for project management include:

- *Gantt chart*: This is a bar chart in which the bars represent the time duration necessary for each individual phase of the project. This chart makes it easier to see where project elements overlap, which elements are dependent on other elements, which need specific personnel, and which will involve the greatest time commitment
- *Network diagram*: A network diagram identifies the various activities in a project and links them graphically through arrows. This diagram shows the sequence of events in a project and how they are interconnected. Network diagrams are also called Critical Path Method (CPM) or Program Evaluation and Review Technique (PERT) charts

Copyright © Mometrix Media. You have been licensed one copy of this document for personal use only. Any other reproduction or redistribution is strictly prohibited. All rights reserved.
This content is provided for test preparation purposes only and does not imply an endorsement by Mometrix of any particular political, scientific, or religious point of view.

Systems Architecture

Systems architecture involves a description of the various elements of a system, including software, hardware, and any other elements and how they are organized. Systems architecture helps define the existing structure of a system and how all its pieces interact, allowing those who make changes to see how a change in one portion of the system might affect other portions of the system. Some types of systems architecture are:

- Collaborative systems
- Social systems
- Manufacturing systems
- Strategic systems
- IT systems

The type of systems architecture used is determined by the function and characteristics of the original system.

SDLC

The Systems Development Life Cycle, or SDLC, is a methodology for information systems development. This methodology uses the systems approach for problem solving and applies it to developing an information system. There are several types of SDLC, from the traditional or waterfall approach to other approaches that have come into use as more companies have made use of the system.

Waterfall Approach to Systems Development

The waterfall approach is also referred to as the traditional SDLC. It makes use of five stages in specific sequence to develop a project:

- *Planning*—planning the project and assembling resources
- *Analysis*—analyzing the system to determine existing problems and needs of the system being developed to deal with those problems
- *Design*—designing the system
- *Implementation*—implementing the system throughout the firm
- *Use*—using the system on a regular basis

This approach represents the most straightforward application of the systems approach to systems development.

Prototyping Approach to Systems Development

The prototyping approach was developed as firms became larger. In the traditional approach, a system would be implemented immediately. The prototype approach allows a system to be tested before full implementation. There are two types of prototypes:

- *Evolutionary prototype*: This prototype evolves over time as developers make changes based on user feedback until the system performs as desired
- *Requirements prototype:* This is not intended to be a representation of the final system, but instead serves to define the new system. Users evaluate the functions of the requirements prototype and add requests for functionality until it meets their needs. Then an additional project begins to develop the final required system

Copyright © Mometrix Media. You have been licensed one copy of this document for personal use only. Any other reproduction or redistribution is strictly prohibited. All rights reserved.
This content is provided for test preparation purposes only and does not imply an endorsement by Mometrix of any particular political, scientific, or religious point of view.

Evolutionary Prototype

There are four steps to developing an evolutionary prototype:

- *Determine the users' needs*: This is usually accomplished via interviews with users
- *Develop the prototype*: This commonly makes use of prototyping tools such as an integrated application generator or a prototyping tool kit. The application generator can produce all of the features of the final system, while the tool kit typically reproduces only some of the features
- *Users judge the prototype's acceptability:* If the prototype does not function as required, the previous steps are repeated until it does
- *Implement the system*: The prototype is adapted as the final system

Developing a Requirements Prototype

The requirements prototype differs from the evolutionary prototype only in the last four steps. The development steps are:

- Determine the users' needs
- Develop the prototype
- Determine the prototype's acceptability
- Write code for the new system based on the prototype
- Test the system with users
- Determine acceptability
- Implement the new system

This approach is typically used for systems that do not require every element of a full-fledged production system.

Prototyping Advantages and Disadvantages

Prototyping helps increase communication between final users and system developers. Because the users are directly involved in the development, the users' needs are often more adequately met, and the users are not taken by surprise when the final system is implemented.

Disadvantages include the possibility of shortcuts that will undermine the effort. Increased expectations due to direct user involvement could lead to disappointment in the final product, and some prototyping tools might not provide the best-quality design.

Overall, prototyping is a highly successful approach to SDLC.

RAD

Rapid Application Development, or RAD, is an SDLC methodology based on the ideas of James Martin, a computer consultant. It focuses on developing systems quickly while maintaining high quality standards. RAD uses information engineering (IE) as its approach to system development. The four vital ingredients in the RAD process are:

- *Management*: The RAD process depends on managers who are willing to experiment with new methods
- *People:* RAD makes use of several specialized teams rather than a single project team. The involvement of users throughout the organization in the process makes RAD a popular choice for many companies

Copyright © Mometrix Media. You have been licensed one copy of this document for personal use only. Any other reproduction or redistribution is strictly prohibited. All rights reserved.
This content is provided for test preparation purposes only and does not imply an endorsement by Mometrix of any particular political, scientific, or religious point of view.

- *Methodologies*: The RAD life cycle drives system development
- *Tools*: Computer-Aided Software Engineering (CASE) tools are used to produce prototypes, code, and databases

Phased Development as a SDLC

Phased development combines the SDLC (Systems Development Life Cycle) approach with prototyping and RAD. The phased development process consists of six stages:

- *Preliminary investigation*: Developers, users, and others analyze the entire system to determine objectives, risks, scope, user requirements, and other elements
- *Analysis:* After gathering user requirements, developers analyze them
- *Design*: Developers design the basic structure of each new required system
- *Preliminary construction*: A test phase during which developers gather feedback from users. Feedback determines whether previous phases must be repeated
- *Final construction*: Integration of the new systems into the old systems on both a software and hardware level.
- *System test and installation*: Full system testing determines the system's functionality and any possible shortcomings. After final approval, the system is put into place, and then its effectiveness is analyzed over time.

BPR

Business Process Redesign (BPR), also known as Business Process Reengineering, often involves redesign of legacy systems, which are systems that are vital to company operations but have been in use long enough that they require more maintenance than is cost-effective or feasible. BPR often causes major changes to a company's infrastructure that lead to a domino effect of redesign throughout other systems. Because of the usually widespread effects of BPR, it is often triggered at a strategic management level. BPR can be applied to almost any part of a company, from an information system to a physical system such as purchasing or human resources. Changes in information systems can trigger changes in physical systems and vice versa.

Two Main Components

The two main components of BPR are:

- *Reverse engineering*: In reverse engineering, programmers analyze an existing system to determine how it works. If a legacy system has been in use for a long time, it is possible that there is not a great deal of documentation about the system, making reverse engineering necessary to determine how it works and how best to retool it
- *Reengineering:* When a system is reengineered, its functionality is changed while keeping the original functionality in mind and maintaining elements as necessary

Whether a system should be completely retooled or just reengineered is determined by the technical quality and functional quality of the existing system. If the system's overall quality is insufficient, forward engineering, or complete retooling of the system, is in order. If either technical or functional quality is still acceptable, other approaches will provide sufficient improvement.

Copyright © Mometrix Media. You have been licensed one copy of this document for personal use only. Any other reproduction or redistribution is strictly prohibited. All rights reserved.
This content is provided for test preparation purposes only and does not imply an endorsement by Mometrix of any particular political, scientific, or religious point of view.

Managing Data Resources

DATA MODELING

Data modeling refers to a model, used most often by software engineers, that defines specific data for a project, how that data is to be used, and the relationships among discrete pieces of data. The meaning of the data is also considered when the data model is built. A data model can be used to develop software, define database models, or define and describe information systems.

Developing a precise, well-defined data model enables everyone working on a project to understand the data and how it is to be used. It helps maintain stability and efficient communication throughout the development process.

ENTERPRISE DATA MODEL

The enterprise data model represents a view of the entire enterprise. All data needed for proper functioning of the firm is determined and eventually stored in a database to be accessed by users who need it. This broad, all-encompassing view of the data within the firm makes the enterprise data model strong and comprehensive. Different problems from different business areas in the firm can be more easily linked, making it easier to share information and solutions between individual business areas. This differs from the process-oriented approach in that the collection of data is not focused on solving a single problem, but on supplying data for the entire company.

ERD

An entity-relationship diagram (ERD) is a way of visualizing data. The diagram shows individual entities and the relationships between these defined entities. Each entity consists of a group of related fields of data.

The ERD shows how various entities should relate to each other. One entity could relate to many others within the diagram. As the ERD is built, these relationships are given names to clarify how the entities interact with each other. After the various entities are placed in the diagram, with all their relationships defined, they can be further defined using data fields that will eventually make up a database.

CLASS DIAGRAMS

Class diagrams are considered object-oriented design models. While an entity-relationship diagram (ERD) shows numerous entities and how they connect to each other throughout the firm, class diagrams show the data as well as actions that must be taken on the data. This collection of information—the data itself, the relationships among the data, and the actions to be taken on the data—comprises an object.

On the simplest level, a class diagram lists the named class, fields within that class, and actions that occur upon the class. Actions are sometimes also called methods. These actions describe how the software or other tool will eventually utilize and/or transform the data.

Copyright © Mometrix Media. You have been licensed one copy of this document for personal use only. Any other reproduction or redistribution is strictly prohibited. All rights reserved.
This content is provided for test preparation purposes only and does not imply an endorsement by Mometrix of any particular political, scientific, or religious point of view.

Database Administrator

The database administrator (DBA) holds an important role in any company that depends on information. The DBA's primary role is to supervise all activities involving the database. These duties include:

- *Database planning*—defining the data needs of end users and selecting database management system software and hardware
- *Database implementation*—creating databases to fulfill the needs of the company and establishing policies and procedures for using the database and keeping the data secure
- *Database operation*—helping and training database users
- *Database security*—maintaining overall security by making sure that those who need the data can access it easily and that those who are not authorized to access the data are denied access to it

Most large companies employ several database administrators.

Database Programmer

The database programmer is a highly trained code developer who creates code to combine, process, or otherwise transform raw data from the database to meet the needs of the company's end users. Programmers also often provide end users with subsets of data that they can then work with on their own workstations. This reduces the load on the database and leads to more efficient database usage overall. The role of database programmer is vital to many end users in the firm, as this employee enables access to necessary data for other employees to do their jobs.

End User

The end user performs numerous tasks using, manipulating, transforming, and processing data supplied by the database. Results of these processes are often used in decision-making processes that affect the whole firm. Database management systems make it easier for the end user to retrieve and manipulate data, as does the work of database programmers within the firm. When a database is constructed, the needs of the end user are vital to determining what data is to be gathered for the database.

Term Database

A database is a repository of data. In a company or firm, the term refers to a collection of information related to a firm's needs. It can mean all information within an entire company, or can refer specifically to that information that is organized through a database management system. In terms of database management, this latter definition is more applicable.

A database typically consists of a variety of data fields. Each data field represents a single piece of information. Several related data fields comprise a record. A collection of related records constitutes a file. A database is a collection of files. The simplest and most common type of database is a spreadsheet.

Copyright © Mometrix Media. You have been licensed one copy of this document for personal use only. Any other reproduction or redistribution is strictly prohibited. All rights reserved.
This content is provided for test preparation purposes only and does not imply an endorsement by Mometrix of any particular political, scientific, or religious point of view.

Hierarchical, Network, and Relations Databases

There are three major types of databases:

- Hierarchical databases were the first types of databases developed. In a hierarchical database, all data is organized in a hierarchical structure, with data groups, subgroups, and more subgroups beneath those. Hierarchical databases are good for some applications that require knowledge about the connections between pieces of data, but are less efficient for retrieving discrete data
- Network databases are focused on retrieving discrete data. However, because every piece of data in a network database is connected to every other piece of data, this type of database can be cumbersome and complex in many applications
- Relational databases are most commonly used in modern businesses. Relationships between tables are determined by overlaps in data that produce implicit relationships

DBMS

Simply put, a database management system (DBMS) is an application designed specifically to manage and organize a database or collection of databases. The DBMS not only stores single databases but also maintains relationships between different pieces of data within that database, and can also generate reports based on the data. The format of each particular piece of data is maintained, and the database itself is placed into an organized and readable format. When a database is controlled by a DBMS, with all the pertinent items of data and data format included, it is sometimes referred to as a self-describing set of related data.

Data Redundancy, Consistency, and Accuracy

Databases are most efficient when data redundancy is reduced and data consistency and accuracy are increased. The use of relational databases helps reduce data redundancy, in which the same information is stored in a variety of different places, often without indication of how it relates to other data. Consistency and accuracy are increased through the use of databases, but are also dependent on accurate data entry and numerous human factors.

Database Concept

The database concept involves the perception that each record in a database is stored consecutively with other related records. To the user's perspective, the database does appear to be consecutive, but in reality individual records can be stored in widely disparate locations. Because the database organizes the information automatically, it appears to be placed in a logical, easily interpreted order.

Terms important to the database concept include:

- *Data independence*: When data is independent, changes can be made to an individual piece of data without affecting the overall organization of the database.
- *Data dictionary*: This is a record that includes definitions of the data within a database. It includes field definitions, table relationships, and other definitions necessary to the basic organization of the database.

Copyright © Mometrix Media. You have been licensed one copy of this document for personal use only. Any other reproduction or redistribution is strictly prohibited. All rights reserved.
This content is provided for test preparation purposes only and does not imply an endorsement by Mometrix of any particular political, scientific, or religious point of view.

Database Creating Process

There are three major phases in the process of creating a database. These are:

- Determining what data must be gathered
- Describing the needed data
- Entering the data

Determining the necessary data to be stored is a vital step and requires planning and communication with end users. Data needs are typically determined through either a process-oriented approach or through enterprise modeling. Both are effective, but they approach this crucial step in slightly different ways.

Process-Oriented Approach

The process-oriented approach is also referred to as a problem-oriented approach, or as process-oriented modeling. It involves a series of steps that must be taken in sequence. These steps are:

- The problem
- The decisions needed to solve the problem
- The information needed for each decision
- Determine the necessary processing to produce the needed information
- Specify the data needed for the necessary processing
- This approach is good for producing a database that must address a specific problem within the firm, whether that problem is a positive or negative change in the firm's function

Enterprise Modeling Approach

An enterprise modeling approach considers all the data needed throughout a firm rather than the data needed to solve a particular problem, as in the process-oriented approach. The enterprise modeling approach works in a top-down sequence, from an extensive enterprise data model that leads to developing the database, and then populating the database with all the necessary information. The enterprise modeling approach allows connections between various data within the firm to be established as the database is put together, and does not isolate certain areas of data from other areas.

Database Management Systems Advantages

There are several advantages to using a DBMS, which is why they have become so extensively utilized in the business world. These advantages include:

- Data redundancy is reduced because the data is compiled into a single source rather than held in numerous places throughout the company
- Data is independent of applications, and can be modified as necessary without affecting the applications
- Data can be retrieved rapidly because of the overall structure of the database
- Data is more secure, since the company database is typically stored separately from individual workstations on a secure server or other location

Copyright © Mometrix Media. You have been licensed one copy of this document for personal use only. Any other reproduction or redistribution is strictly prohibited. All rights reserved.
This content is provided for test preparation purposes only and does not imply an endorsement by Mometrix of any particular political, scientific, or religious point of view.

Database Management Systems Disadvantages

Although a database management system is a very efficient and popular way to organize and store a company's data, there are some disadvantages, including:

- Most database management systems are expensive, making them difficult for some smaller companies to implement
- Because the database is usually accessed by a large number of people within the company, the hardware on which it is stored must be powerful and able to handle this load on its systems
- To fully utilize a database management system requires a specialized database administration staff, representing another large expense

Query and QBE

A database query is a way for an end user to ask the database a direct question. The end user can request that specific records are displayed through an interface in the DBMS. The query itself specifies the required data fields and displays only those records that fit the specifications.

A commonly used form of query is query-by-example, or QBE. In QBE, the DBMS generates a form the end user can use to specify the required data. The DBMS then uses the example provided by the form to retrieve the requested information.

SQL

SQL, or structured query language, is a computer language or code used within relational database management systems. SQL forms the basis of most databases found on the web, and is an integral part of any online function that must retrieve data from a database, such as an online store. The storefront uses SQL to query the store's database and return records requested by the customer, whether those records are requested through a site search or a request to add an item to a shopping cart. SQL is relatively simple as a language, but serves as a powerful tool in managing databases.

OLAP

Online analytical processing, or OLAP, enables rapid data retrieval and analysis. Rather than using a large number of queries to retrieve data, OLAP tools provide data in a structure that is depicted to the user as a cube. Relationships between various types of data in the cube can be retrieved from any perspective or dimension of the cube, such as subtotals, combinations of various categories, or other complex data interactions. OLAP provides this information quickly and efficiently. Most DBMSs today provide some sort of OLAP browsing. Microsoft Excel provides another tool called a pivot table that serves as an interface to the OLAP cube. OLAP applications typically retrieve data from a data warehouse.

ROLAP and MOLAP

ROLAP and MOLAP are different approaches to OLAP. ROLAP stands for relational online analytical processing. ROLAP makes use of a relational DBMS when processing data. Multidimensional online analytical processing, or MOLAP, uses a specially designed multidimensional DBMS.

ROLAP data generally must be analyzed and processed into summaries to be used easily by end users. ROLAP, then, is limited to a certain number of dimensions. MOLAP pre-processes data to produce usable summaries for the end user. Because of its pre-processing and ability to create summaries, MOLAP can create reports with ten or more dimensions.

Copyright © Mometrix Media. You have been licensed one copy of this document for personal use only. Any other reproduction or redistribution is strictly prohibited. All rights reserved.
This content is provided for test preparation purposes only and does not imply an endorsement by Mometrix of any particular political, scientific, or religious point of view.

FORMS

A form typically displays single records. These records usually are not aggregated, nor are summary data provided regarding the records. Forms can provide these types of information, but usually do not.

The main function of a form, rather, is to add, modify, or delete database records. Using a form, an end user can easily enter information that will be added to the database without having to access the database directly. Forms provide easy-to-use access for the end user while also providing protection to the database overall, since forms work with only one record at a time.

FIVE ELEMENTS OF FORMS

Five major elements are important to the ease of use of a form:

- *Navigation:* The user can move from record to record quickly, usually using a navigation toolbar.
- *Accuracy:* Fields within forms are pre-populated with parameters that define what can be entered in each field. For example, if a field for a course code must have only alphanumeric values, the form will not allow entry of any other types of characters
- *Consistency*: Forms can provide drop-down menus of frequently used fields or other ways of automatically populating a field for data commonly placed in that field, reducing the risk of mistyping
- *Filtering:* This allows the end user to narrow down the data being viewed
- *Sub-forms*: Allowing forms to connect to and interact with each other via sub-forms allows even more flexibility with the data that can be entered

REPORTS AND FORMS IMPORTANCE TO END USERS

Reports and forms are the most common ways for an end user to interact with a company database. These aggregations of data are used to answer specific questions, solve business problems, or monitor the performance of the company, from individual systems to the entire firm. Reports and forms organize data from the database in such a way that it can be easily interpreted and understood by end users, helping them do their jobs more efficiently and also helping them acquire necessary information quickly so that time and resources are conserved. Database administrators and database programmers work to ensure that the databases contain the information end users will need, and that end users can retrieve that data easily and in a form relevant to their needs. A form or report is usually the most efficient way to achieve this goal.

REPORTS

Reports differ from forms in that they usually process the data in some way. Data is organized and then aggregated in a format specified by the end user. The data can then be used to make decisions about various company matters or to judge performance levels of different parts of the firm.

End users must be aware of how a particular DBMS processes data in order to use reports efficiently. In some cases, the default settings in a DBMS will exclude important data for a particular report, requiring the end user to change the defaults to properly represent a specific data set and achieve the appropriate results.

GUI IMPORTANCE IN A DBMS

A GUI (graphical user interface) is the most easily interpreted and readily used way of accessing a database. The majority of DBMSs (database management system) make use of a GUI so that end users can intuitively work with the data without requiring extensive training. Use of a DBMS does

Copyright © Mometrix Media. You have been licensed one copy of this document for personal use only. Any other reproduction or redistribution is strictly prohibited. All rights reserved.
This content is provided for test preparation purposes only and does not imply an endorsement by Mometrix of any particular political, scientific, or religious point of view.

require practice and familiarity with the particular application, but a well-constructed GUI makes the learning curve much less steep. With an intuitive GUI, even a first-time user can often use the DBMS right away. Since many end users who need access to the company database are not DBMS specialists, the GUI makes it much easier and more efficient for data to be disseminated throughout the company.

Copyright © Mometrix Media. You have been licensed one copy of this document for personal use only. Any other reproduction or redistribution is strictly prohibited. All rights reserved.
This content is provided for test preparation purposes only and does not imply an endorsement by Mometrix of any particular political, scientific, or religious point of view.

Business Decision Making

CSF

A CSF, or a critical success factor, is an area in a company that must function well in order for the company to succeed. The term was coined in 1961 by Ronald Daniel. CSFs vary from one company to another, depending on that company's needs. Companies will often focus major resources on monitoring CSFs and how these particular areas are performing.

With the growing use of information technology, information has become a valuable asset to large companies, and a powerful information management system is considered a CSF. A company that can use expert knowledge management to increase efficiency will have a competitive advantage.

TRANSACTION PROCESSING SYSTEM

Transaction processing system is a generic name for the specific information system in a company that gathers necessary data, processes it, and makes it easily accessible to end users. Other terms that describe basically the same thing are electronic data processing system and accounting information system. These terms have fallen out of popularity.

In the transaction processing system, data is gathered from throughout the firm's physical systems and placed in the database. The data can then be retrieved by anyone who needs it, whether they are inside or outside the company. This includes data for customers as well as internal personnel. Each company formulates its own transaction processing system to meet its specific needs.

DISTRIBUTION SYSTEM

A distribution system is a type of transaction processing system that performs the specific function of delivering products or services to a company's customers. These products can be in the form of tangible goods as in the case of a retailer or wholesaler, or in the form of services such as those provided by a hospital or a government agency. Regardless of a company's main purpose or product, nearly all companies function as distributors in some way or another.

As with transaction processing system, distribution system is a generic term. Each individual company develops its own distribution system based on what the company needs.

MAJOR SUBSYSTEMS

There are three basic subsystems of a distribution system, which perform the following tasks:

- Fill orders. When a customer orders a product, the system will fulfill that order. Subsystems that handle this task include the order-entry system, inventory system, billing system, and accounts receivable system
- Order stock to maintain inventory. These systems ensure that enough product is available for the customers, and include the purchasing system, receiving system, and accounts payable system
- Maintain the general ledger. The general-ledger system performs accounting tasks by combining accounting information from across the firm. Systems include the update-general-ledger system and the prepare-management-reports system

ORGANIZATIONAL INFORMATION SYSTEMS

Within a company, a different information system is usually developed for each business area. Business areas include human resources, manufacturing, marketing, finance, and information

Copyright © Mometrix Media. You have been licensed one copy of this document for personal use only. Any other reproduction or redistribution is strictly prohibited. All rights reserved.
This content is provided for test preparation purposes only and does not imply an endorsement by Mometrix of any particular political, scientific, or religious point of view.

services. The information systems developed for each area are collectively referred to as organizational information systems. The five major types are:

- Marketing information system (MKIS)
- Human resources information system (HRIS)
- Manufacturing information system
- Financial information system
- Executive information system (EIS)

Each of these systems manages information within the defined business area.

Basic Structure

MKIS example: The MKIS, like all organizational information systems, consists of three elements:

- Output subsystems provide information about specific data that management must monitor. In the MKIS, this information consists of four elements: the product subsystem, promotion subsystem, price subsystem (these three are referred to as the marketing mix), and the integrated-mix subsystem (which combines the other three elements)
- Input subsystems gather data from the firm and the firm's environment, and place the data in the database. The MKIS uses the marketing research subsystem and the marketing intelligence subsystem to achieve this goal
- The database is the repository of all relevant data for the system

EIS

The EIS, sometimes referred to as the executive support system, or ESS, provides information to managers in a firm. Typical information supplied involves reports about the company's performance, profits and other data necessary to make executive-level decisions.

Generally, the hardware components of an EIS include a central computer that is connected to executive workstations. Individual workstations often have secondary storage with a database specifically constructed for executive-level users. The information in this database is preprocessed to meet executives' needs, and executives can use preformatted displays to produce reports. When an executive prefers more detailed data rather than high-level summaries, the EIS provides drill-down capability to allow lower-level data views.

CRM

Most information systems focus on a limited timeframe for their data, usually maintaining data within the company's fiscal year. Customer relationship management (CRM), however, maintains long-term historical data to help better serve customers. CRM is aimed at maintaining quality relationships between the company and its customers, and retaining customers over a long period of time. CRM typically makes use of a data warehouse to maintain data that is instrumental in helping the company meet the various needs of its customers. CRM also combines customer contact information from a variety of different sources and can also supply an interface for customers to manage their own data and interaction with the company.

Copyright © Mometrix Media. You have been licensed one copy of this document for personal use only. Any other reproduction or redistribution is strictly prohibited. All rights reserved.
This content is provided for test preparation purposes only and does not imply an endorsement by Mometrix of any particular political, scientific, or religious point of view.

Data Warehouse

"Data warehouse" refers to a type of data storage system. The exact system varies from company to company, but carries a set of characteristics:

- The system's storage capacity is extremely large
- Data within the system is easily retrieved
- Data records increase as users add new records rather than by updating records already in the system
- Data is not used for day-to-day operations, but instead for making various business decisions

When a company sets about to create a data warehouse, often it does so in smaller chunks due to the necessarily large nature of a full data warehouse. These small sections are referred to as data marts. Typically, a data mart represents data focused on a specific business area such as human resources. The system that develops around using a data warehouse is called data warehousing. The data warehouse is managed through a DBMS.

ETL Process

ETL stands for extraction, transformation, and loading. This refers to a process within the data warehousing system. Data is gathered from the company and external sources, then assembled in a staging area and evaluated before being entered into the data warehouse. ETL occurs in this staging area and consists of:

- *Extraction*: Data from all the relevant sources is combined
- *Transformation*: Data is cleaned, formatted, and summarized. This ensures that the data is presented in a standardized manner and makes it easier to access and understand
- *Loading*: The final step, in which the gathered data is entered into the data warehouse

In addition to providing data for the data warehouse, metadata is also provided. Metadata is literally data about the data, and functions as a description of data within the warehouse as well as a way of tracking data flow throughout the system.

Data Warehousing Importance

Data warehousing allows a company to keep track of massive amounts of data regarding sales patterns, marketing campaigns, customer interaction, and anything else the company needs to track in order to evaluate and make decisions about current and future operations. Until the use of large, powerful computers became commonplace within a company, this kind of information was extremely difficult if not impossible to maintain over long periods of time. It required a huge paper trail and many people to work with the information. With data warehousing, a theoretically unlimited amount of long-term data is easily stored, compiled, and summarized for use by managers and others who need it in the course of performing their jobs.

Changing the Way a Company Thinks About Its Data

Data warehousing does not focus on keeping on file current data about a company's operations. Rather, it is simply a way to accumulate large quantities of data that can then be compiled into reports, evaluated in various ways, and applied to company-wide decision making. Data is not transformed through updates, but instead is simply added to as the company grows and changes. This massive accumulation of data can show end users how a company has changed over time, and how certain decisions have helped or hindered company operations. Data from a data warehouse

Copyright © Mometrix Media. You have been licensed one copy of this document for personal use only. Any other reproduction or redistribution is strictly prohibited. All rights reserved.
This content is provided for test preparation purposes only and does not imply an endorsement by Mometrix of any particular political, scientific, or religious point of view.

not only can provide information about current trends, but also can look at trends as they have developed over the life of the company.

THREE TYPES OF DATA

Three major types of data are stored in a data warehouse:

- Identifying data such as a number assigned to a customer or inventory item
- Descriptive data such as a customer or product name
- Quantitative data such as number of sales of a certain product or for a certain time period

TWO TABLES USED TO STORE THAT DATA

This data, when entered into the data warehouse, is stored in two different types of tables:

- *Dimension tables*: These tables store the identifying data and the descriptive data. This usually consists of an identifying number or code as well as other information tied to that code, like a customer's name, address, and email or a product's description, dimensions, or price
- *Fact tables:* Quantitative data is stored in the fact tables. Fact tables hold information about specific activities such as sales and various data related to sales, like commissions, taxes, bonuses, or other vital data

INFORMATION PACKAGES

With identifying and descriptive data stored in dimension tables and quantitative data stored in fact tables, the data warehousing system must associate a dimension table with its matching fact table. To do this, the system combines the tables into an information package, which contains all the identifying, descriptive, and quantitative data for any particular activity. With this information, an end user can analyze the data from numerous dimensions.

Within the information package is a key, usually the identifying data (a number or code referring to a customer, for example), and any number of additional dimensions. The additional dimensions are pieces of data describing the key. An end user can group these pieces of data in numerous ways for evaluation.

STAR SCHEMA WORK

A star schema is another way to present data to the end user. A star schema connects dimension tables to fact tables, rather than connecting fact tables to dimension tables as does an information package. This allows pieces of data to be connected to each other in various ways such that a graphic representation of the connections resembles a star. The star schema allows a relational database to present data in a multidimensional way without requiring a special multidimensional database management system. It gives end users much more flexibility in the way they can view and analyze data from within the data warehouse.

THREE COMPANY TYPES THAT COULD BENEFIT FROM DATA WAREHOUSING

Technically, any company can benefit from data warehousing. Different companies will store different types of data and analyze it in different ways, but the ability to store huge quantities of data over time can revolutionize the way any business makes its decisions.

Copyright © Mometrix Media. You have been licensed one copy of this document for personal use only. Any other reproduction or redistribution is strictly prohibited. All rights reserved.
This content is provided for test preparation purposes only and does not imply an endorsement by Mometrix of any particular political, scientific, or religious point of view.

Companies often cited as examples for using data warehousing include:

- Companies that rely on direct sales to customers. Data warehousing helps store information about individual customers, sales trends, results of marketing efforts, and other important data about the company
- Companies that provide direct services to customers. Maintaining data about individual customers helps these companies provide more individualized service
- Companies that must track commission sales for a sales staff. Data warehousing helps identify trends over time, efficiency of individual sales teams, and other vital statistics

DATA MINING

Data mining is a function related to data warehousing in which an automated process searches through data looking for specific relationships. Users may or may not be aware of these relationships—often data mining is used to discover relationships the user has not yet found. The data mining process finds these relationships and then presents them to the user in such a way that the user can easily view and analyze the resulting data.

Data mining has become more and more important in larger companies as techniques have become more refined. Early data mining often returned data that did not accurately represent the desired relationships, or data that was for the most part meaningless. More sophisticated data mining processes have made this a vital part of the data warehousing system for any company.

HYPOTHESIS VERIFICATION

A traditional approach to database query, hypothesis verification retrieves data from the data warehouse based on specific requests by the user. The user inputs certain criteria for the data he or she wishes to retrieve. These criteria can represent several dimensions of the desired data. Based on the request, the system returns lists of data. For example, the user might ask for customers that fit a certain demographic.

The process is referred to as hypothesis verification because the data returned is based on the hypothesis by the user that this data will be the best suited for his eventual use. A user might hypothesize that a certain marketing effort will appeal most to women between the ages of 35 and 45, and thus request that information. The strength of the data returned to solve the problem is directly related to the user's hypothesis.

KNOWLEDGE DISCOVERY

Knowledge discovery requires the data warehousing system to be able to analyze the data beyond the requests of an individual user. This type of data mining makes use of processes that can find data for a specific request that the user might not have thought to request. Rather than responding to very specific criteria, the software that mines the data will use patterns it perceives in the data to return a wider variety of data than the user might have initially anticipated. For example, a query the user might have thought would be most applicable to women aged 35 to 45 might also return data on men aged 45 to 55 because the software sees similar spending patterns in this group. Knowledge discovery uses artificial intelligence tools to make these connections.

NAVIGATING DATA TABLE OR DATABASE TERMS

These terms all refer to different ways of navigating through a data table or a database system:

- *Drill down*: Drill down refers to the process of navigating down through a hierarchy of data
- *Drill across*: Navigating horizontally from one hierarchy of data to another

Copyright © Mometrix Media. You have been licensed one copy of this document for personal use only. Any other reproduction or redistribution is strictly prohibited. All rights reserved.
This content is provided for test preparation purposes only and does not imply an endorsement by Mometrix of any particular political, scientific, or religious point of view.

- *Drill through*: Moving from higher-level, summary data to lower-level, detailed data
- *Roll up*: Moving from a lower-level, detailed view up through levels that summarize the data

Multidimensional Analysis

Multidimensional analysis allows data to be analyzed from the perspective of many different dimensions or perspectives. The term usually refers to the use of three or more dimensions. For example, analyzing the number of customers who bought a specific product over a certain period of time would represent three different data dimensions. This kind of complex analysis provides high-quality information to end users who use the data for decision making within the company.

Multidimensional analysis is sometimes accomplished in a company's data warehouse using specially designed multidimensional database management systems, or MOLAP (multidimensional online analytical processing). However, these systems are quite expensive. A less expensive way to accomplish multidimensional analysis is using star schema with a relational database.

Copyright © Mometrix Media. You have been licensed one copy of this document for personal use only. Any other reproduction or redistribution is strictly prohibited. All rights reserved.
This content is provided for test preparation purposes only and does not imply an endorsement by Mometrix of any particular political, scientific, or religious point of view.

MIS and the Organization

Information System's Use

Anyone in a company can be an end user of information. When computers were first introduced into the business sphere, the most frequent users were those in the accounting department, as well as some managers. Computer output consisted more of data than of information. As computers came to be used more widely, more and more employees in the company used them, and the emphasis shifted as use expanded from just collecting data to gathering information and processing it to support business decision making. Managerial use became more widespread. In today's companies, managers make extensive use of information to make short-term and long-term decisions in every aspect of the business. Non-managers also use information to support their own work responsibilities.

Three Major Management Levels

The three management levels perform different functions in a company. Their functions determine how they use information and information systems.

- *Strategic planning level*: This is considered the top management level, and usually refers to the president and vice president of a company. Their decisions affect the strategic plans of a company on a large scale, often planning years of company strategy at a time.
- *Management control level*: This is mid-level management, and includes division heads, regional managers, and product directors. These managers execute plans and make sure the company meets its overall goals.
- *Operational control level*: These are lower-level managers who lead specific projects or departments, or supervise smaller groups of people. These managers run the company's day-to-day operations.

Five Major Business Areas

The three traditional business areas are:

- *Marketing*: Brings information about products and services to consumers
- *Manufacturing*: Produces the product that is sold
- *Finance:* Manages the day-to-day flow of money into and out of the company

Two additional areas that are relatively new to the business world are:

- *Human resources*: Hires and fires employees and manages various employee benefits as well as interactions between employees and managers
- *Information services*: Provides data and information to the entire company and maintains hardware and software elements of the company's information systems

Five Major Functions of Management

The five major functions of management were defined in 1914 by Henri Fayol, a French management theorist. These roles were defined as:

- *Plan*: Decide what their part of the organization will do to meet a goal
- *Organize*: Decide how best to meet that goal
- *Staff:* Acquire resources and employees to accomplish the goal

Copyright © Mometrix Media. You have been licensed one copy of this document for personal use only. Any other reproduction or redistribution is strictly prohibited. All rights reserved.
This content is provided for test preparation purposes only and does not imply an endorsement by Mometrix of any particular political, scientific, or religious point of view.

- *Direct*: Tell the employees how to accomplish the decided goal
- *Control*: Keep the project team focused on the project's goal

Later theorists determined that these five roles were too generalized, and developed another set of ten managerial roles.

Ten Major Managerial Roles

There are also ten major managerial roles, developed by Henry Mintzberg, which fall into three different categories:

Interpersonal roles

- *Figurehead*—represents the company
- *Leader*—leads a team of employees
- *Liaison*—makes connections both inside and outside the company

Informational roles

- *Monitor*—watches out for information relative to his or her project
- *Disseminator*—passes information along to those who need it
- *Spokesperson*—represents his or her group to others in the company

Decisional roles

- *Entrepreneur*—makes improvements to his or her group
- *Disturbance handler*—manages unexpected challenges
- *Resource allocator*—decides who in the group gets what resources
- *Negotiator*—resolves disputes within the group and between the group and others

Problem solving and decision making

In business, a problem is defined as any situation that could be either harmful or beneficial to the company. Problem solving involves determining the best way to prevent a harmful situation or encourage a beneficial situation. The determined course of action is the solution.

To solve any individual problem, a manager or team must make a series of decisions to determine exactly what the problem is, what possible ways exist to solve it, and which solutions will lead to the best outcome. The decision-making process is aided and supported by information systems that provide sufficient information and data to the manager or group to help them make the best decision regarding a course of action.

Four major problem-solving phases

Management scientist Herbert A. Simon defined four generalized phases to solving any problem:

- *Intelligence activity*: Finding and defining existing problems
- *Design activity*: Determining all available courses of action to address individual problems
- *Choice activity*: Deciding which course of action will lead to the best overall solution
- *Review activity:* Assessing the results of the decided course of action

Each of these phases requires information, provided by the management information systems within the company. Since MIS supports decision making, it is a vital part of any company's resources.

Copyright © Mometrix Media. You have been licensed one copy of this document for personal use only. Any other reproduction or redistribution is strictly prohibited. All rights reserved.
This content is provided for test preparation purposes only and does not imply an endorsement by Mometrix of any particular political, scientific, or religious point of view.

ANTICIPATED FUTURE CHANGES TO MIS

MIS continues to change every day as information becomes less expensive and more easily available. Rapidly advancing technology puts unprecedented amounts of information at the fingertips of everyone who has a computer, cell phone, or other mobile device. These devices continue to become more sophisticated and more available to everyday users.

Where information was once limited to those who could afford it, now it is available free of charge via the Internet and even traditional library systems. Information is also more easily available to companies and managers, so that decisions made based on this information can be more accurate and effective, with endless possibilities, provided that those using the information interpret it carefully and do not succumb to data overload.

DIFFERENT LEVELS OF MANAGEMENT INFORMATION

Each level of management maintains a specific focus depending on its overall responsibilities. Higher-level management tends to require higher-level, summary data that has been processed in specific ways to provide information that affects the entire company.

Lower-level managers will look for information at a lower level that provides feedback on how their particular projects are performing. Management information systems must be able to provide data for all levels of management, from high-level overviews to lower-level information about specific projects and individual departments. The increasing power of information systems makes it possible to provide the necessary flexibility to provide all levels of management in a company with exactly the type of information they need.

THREE DIMENSIONS OF COMPETITIVE ADVANTAGE

There are three basic dimensions to competitive advantage, and MIS can provide an edge in all of these.

- *Strategic advantage*: MIS can provide information to help upper-level managers determine how to improve the company's overall direction
- *Tactical advantage*: The company can determine how to implement specific strategies more efficiently than competitors
- *Operational advantage*: MIS can improve day-to-day processes, making them more efficient

MIS provides information to managers at all levels, helping them determine the best way to run the company and perform better than industry competitors.

SUPPLY CHAIN MANAGEMENT

The supply chain is the series of events that must take place in order for a company's goods and services to flow from suppliers to customers. Supply chain management is the management of these events. Activities in the supply chain are:

- Predicting demand for the product
- Determining a production schedule to meet demand
- Setting up transportation networks to deliver product
- Acquiring additional products from suppliers
- Receiving products shipped from suppliers
- Inventory management at all levels of production

Copyright © Mometrix Media. You have been licensed one copy of this document for personal use only. Any other reproduction or redistribution is strictly prohibited. All rights reserved.
This content is provided for test preparation purposes only and does not imply an endorsement by Mometrix of any particular political, scientific, or religious point of view.

MIS Four Dimensions of Information

All information carries four basic dimensions that contribute to the information's value to the firm:

- *Relevance*: Information is more valuable when it directly relates to the firm's functions and needs
- *Accuracy*: Accuracy is most important in financial applications. Other applications for information, such as trend forecasting, do not require perfect accuracy
- *Timeliness:* The availability of extensive, accurate information before a crisis occurs can alert managers to potential problems in time to avert the crisis
- *Completeness*: MIS should be able to provide a full, complete picture of any aspect of the firm. However, users should be able to limit this picture to their own needs to prevent information overload, which can obscure possible solutions to problems or make it hard to see where problems might be developing

MIS Strategic Planning Support

Strategic planning occurs at the highest management level of a company. Typically, this function is performed by the CEO, or chief executive officer, and other members of a company's executive committee, including those in charge of the company's individual business areas. MIS provides information for these executives to make decisions regarding the overall strategic plan for the entire company. Often the CIO, or chief information officer, is also involved in strategic planning. This officer oversees MIS throughout the company and ensures that MIS provides appropriate and necessary information to all departments.

Producing the Product

Delivering the product to customers, tracking the product through the entire production/delivery process, every step of the supply chain can be enhanced and improved through MIS.

SPIR

Strategic planning for information resources (SPIR) represents the development of a strategic plan for a company's information services that is integrated with the company's overall strategic plan. Where the company's overall plans require support from information systems, plans are put into place so that the information resources department can ensure it has enough infrastructures in place, as regards both hardware and personnel, to meet those needs. Each set of systems within the company should determine its information needs based on its own strategic plans so that the SPIR process can accommodate those plans. The more closely various groups in the corporation can work with MIS and those in charge of MIS, the better their needs will be met.

Copyright © Mometrix Media. You have been licensed one copy of this document for personal use only. Any other reproduction or redistribution is strictly prohibited. All rights reserved.
This content is provided for test preparation purposes only and does not imply an endorsement by Mometrix of any particular political, scientific, or religious point of view.

MIS Issues

MIS ISSUES

One challenge faced by MIS is digital rights to various types of data. While much information is free for the taking, other information is protected by copyright, digital rights management, or other rules and regulations regarding intellectual property. This is of particular concern to companies that deal with digital products such as music or electronic books.

The firm must maintain a balance between protecting its own product and meeting the needs of the consumer. MIS can help determine customer needs so the firm can respond to these needs by changing price structures, making products available in different formats, or other actions indicated by consumer response and various sales trends.

DATA BACKUP TO MIS

Any MIS security plan should include data backup. Because MIS contains such a large amount of company information, especially if the company uses a data warehouse, the loss of this data could constitute a severe blow to the company's ability to remain in business.

There are many ways to back up information. The most effective way is to back data up to a location that can be stored off-site or that is off-site to begin with. Remote servers, either owned by the company or by a data backup service, provide a reliable off-site location to back up a company's data. In case of a catastrophic event at the company site, such as a fire or massive server failure, the data will then be safe. Backup can be scheduled to occur automatically, making even extensive backup a simple process.

UPS

UPS stands for uninterrupted power supply. The UPS is basically a battery that is kept connected to the electrical supply in order to maintain a constant charge. Computers and computer equipment are plugged into the UPS. In cases of power outage, the computers remain powered up through the UPS, preventing catastrophic data loss due to abrupt shutdown. The UPS typically provides sufficient power to keep a computer running through a short-term power loss, and enough time to shut the computer down properly during a longer loss of power.

SECURITY AUDITS

Security audits help determine who has access to what data, what kind of computer activity has taken place, and how consistently employees adhere to security guidelines throughout the company. Periodic security audits can protect management information systems by ensuring that proprietary data is protected by current security measures. Actions can be taken if security has been breached, such as changes in personnel or changes to security guidelines and procedures.

Audits tend to be time-consuming and expensive, so an individual company must determine whether the likely benefits outweigh the possible cost and inevitable disruption to everyday company operations.

HIRING POLICIES AND EMPLOYEE EVALUATION

Hiring trustworthy employees is important in maintaining a secure company environment overall. Companies can check prospective employees for criminal records or other possible problems.

Copyright © Mometrix Media. You have been licensed one copy of this document for personal use only. Any other reproduction or redistribution is strictly prohibited. All rights reserved.
This content is provided for test preparation purposes only and does not imply an endorsement by Mometrix of any particular political, scientific, or religious point of view.

It is also important to evaluate employees from time to time to ensure they are following established company security measures. In some cases, companies will monitor employees' activities online on a daily basis, even going so far as to track keystrokes during regular work tasks.

The best way to ensure security among employees is to maintain an atmosphere where employees are happy and willing to follow security requirements. Security policies that are too strict can create an atmosphere where employees feel that they are not trusted.

CODE OF ETHICS

A code of ethics helps establish the ethics culture of a company by defining ethical behavior and the types of behavior expected from employees in various circumstances. Several organizations, including the Association for Computing Machinery (ACM), have defined ethics codes that can be used and adapted for specific companies. The ACM's ethics codes provide a comprehensive template for company codes of ethics regarding moral imperatives, work ethics, leadership, and code compliance across the board. A code of ethics can hold employees to a high standard of behavior, thus improving the security of MIS and the company in general.

ACM CODE OF ETHICS

The Association for Computing Machinery (ACM) lists four major imperatives in its Code of Ethics and Professional Conduct:

- *General Moral Imperatives*—related to overall moral behavior as well as issues directly related to information systems such as intellectual property, confidentiality, and privacy
- *More Specific Professional Responsibilities*—related to professional conduct and social responsibilities of the profession
- *Organizational Leadership Imperatives*—help others meet their responsibilities, help the organization benefit from information systems, and protect users' interest
- *Compliance with the Code*—overall support for the Code of Ethics in general

Computer professionals working within corporations or in their own companies can use the ACM Code of Ethics as a guideline for their own ethical conduct.

ACM SOFTWARE ENGINEERING CODE OF ETHICS

The ACM also has a Code of Ethics aimed specifically at software engineers. This code discusses expectations of ethical conduct in eight areas:

- *Public*: The engineer's work should be in the public interest
- *Client and Employer:* The engineer should act in the employer's best interests without violating the public interest
- *Product*: The product should meet the highest possible industry standards
- *Judgment*: The engineer should exercise independent professional judgment while maintaining personal integrity
- *Management*: Engineers are to use ethical methods in managing software products
- *Profession*: Engineers should provide a positive view of their profession to the public
- *Colleagues:* The engineer should support his or her colleagues and deal with them fairly
- *Self*: The engineer should spend time on self-improvement and learning throughout his or her career

Copyright © Mometrix Media. You have been licensed one copy of this document for personal use only. Any other reproduction or redistribution is strictly prohibited. All rights reserved.
This content is provided for test preparation purposes only and does not imply an endorsement by Mometrix of any particular political, scientific, or religious point of view.

EDUCATION IN COMPUTER ETHICS

Three main sources of education in computer ethics are:

- *Colleges*: Universities, colleges, and business schools offer a variety of courses in computer ethics. Courses are also available through online educators
- *Professional programs*: These are offered by professional organizations such as the American Management Association
- *Private programs*: Several organizations offer private courses in computer ethics and other important issues. Courses can be tailored to the specific needs of a company and presented in-house or in special presentations for that company's employees

CIO ROLE IN PROMOTING ETHICS

The CIO (chief information officer) can assist the company in meeting federal guidelines that require executives to sign off on financial statements. Ways in which the CIO can assist this effort include:

- Help involved personnel understand accounting principles in general
- Work to ensure that information systems involved in financial reporting and transaction process work properly and accurately
- Be involved in the processes by which stockholders and others are given financial information about the company
- Allow information systems to warn executives when issues develop in the financial areas of the company
- Ensure executives understand the company's financial systems
- Control the portion of the budget that supports information systems

PROTECTING PERSONAL PRIVACY ONLINE

There are several ways to protect personal information while using online services. One way is to be sure that any companies, off-line or online, do not distribute personal data to other companies or organizations. Individuals can refuse to give personal information to companies or stop doing business with them if they insist on collecting too much personal data. It is also possible to look at any personal information and request that inaccuracies be corrected. This includes credit reports that might have inaccurate data that could affect credit scores. Particularly sensitive data, such as credit card numbers and social security numbers, should be treated with extra caution.

US PRIVACY LAWS OVERVIEW

Privacy laws in the US are sparse at the federal level. Some states have stronger laws. Laws change from time to time as technology makes private information easier to access. Certain data such as medical data, library and video rental data, school grades, and driver's license information are all protected by various regulations. Credit data can be acquired by individuals, but a fee is usually required. Medical and student information can be released only with permission from the patient or student. Protection for other information such as credit card data, addresses, and data used for purchasing goods online is provided largely by the seller. Bank information for online banking is protected by the banks. However, companies can still purchase email lists from which to build a customer base.

EU PRIVACY LAWS

In the European Union (EU), laws protecting consumer privacy are more extensive than in the US These laws are largely based on the 1995 Data Protection Directive. Some elements of these laws

Copyright © Mometrix Media. You have been licensed one copy of this document for personal use only. Any other reproduction or redistribution is strictly prohibited. All rights reserved.
This content is provided for test preparation purposes only and does not imply an endorsement by Mometrix of any particular political, scientific, or religious point of view.

specify that data cannot be transferred to a country with less-strict protection guidelines. This includes the US, though the US has made arrangements with the EU that allow data transfer if the individual company follows directives from the EU and promises not to sell the data. Selling customer lists is generally illegal in Europe, though it is common practice in the US

Internet Issues of Anonymity

Advanced technology has made it possible to use the Internet without divulging any private information at all. For those who feel strongly about protecting their private information, this can be a reasonable if sometimes complicated option. However, if anonymity is used to hide illegal activity, harassment, or other inappropriate behavior, the same advanced technology can gather enough information to trace the individual responsible. This usually requires a court order. Debate about whether anonymity on the Internet should be allowed and under what circumstances continues as different factions discuss the various implications.

MNC

A multinational corporation, or MNC, typically has a parent company and subsidiary companies that work out of different parts of the world. This type of corporation often handles a wide range of products and services in a variety of countries. Many modern companies outsource work to other countries such as India and China to cut costs, meaning that a large part of a specific department of the company could be working out of a country different from that of the parent company. Information technology is particularly important to an MNC to help coordinate the work of the various subsidiaries with that of the parent company.

Drawbacks include language and cultural barriers as well as differing laws governing intellectual property rights, which could endanger the company's vital information systems.

GIS and Some Political Constraints

A global information system, or GIS, is an information system made up of various international networks. This kind of information system provides its own unique set of challenges. Because the logistics of a GIS are so complicated, a well-defined company strategy is necessary to make it successful.

One challenge of a GIS involves politics. When networks cross borders, political issues must be considered. In some countries, it may prove difficult to ensure that a subsidiary can easily access the network. High-speed networks are not available everywhere, and often are much more difficult to access in other countries. Often the communications network is managed by a country's government rather than by private companies, adding additional challenges to setting up a GIS.

GIS Cultural and Communications Issues

In order to be effective, a GIS (global information system) must be usable by all employees, even those who use a different language than that used at the parent company. GISs often make use of graphical interfaces to make the interface more flexible. Attitudes toward IT work vary in different

Copyright © Mometrix Media. You have been licensed one copy of this document for personal use only. Any other reproduction or redistribution is strictly prohibited. All rights reserved.
This content is provided for test preparation purposes only and does not imply an endorsement by Mometrix of any particular political, scientific, or religious point of view.

cultures as well. Employees at subsidiary companies might find technology-based work less respected than it is in the US, for example. Other possible GIS issues include:

- *Hardware restrictions*: Local governments might require use of locally manufactured hardware and software
- *Data processing restrictions*: Rules might require data to be processed locally rather than transmitted out of the country
- *Data flow restrictions*: TDF, or transborder data flow, has become an issue, restricting the flow of electronic data across international borders as a privacy measure

MNC

A multinational corporation, or MNC, typically has a parent company and subsidiary companies that work out of different parts of the world. This type of corporation often handles a wide range of products and services in a variety of countries. Many modern companies outsource work to other countries such as India and China to cut costs, meaning that a large part of a specific department of the company could be working out of a country different from that of the parent company. Information technology is particularly important to an MNC to help coordinate the work of the various subsidiaries with that of the parent company.

Drawbacks include language and cultural barriers as well as differing laws governing intellectual property rights, which could endanger the company's vital information systems.

GIS TECHNOLOGY ISSUES

A successful GIS depends on available technology in the countries in which the subsidiaries function. Since access to technology and various elements that support it are not the same in all countries, this can become a challenge as the GIS is being developed. Some technological issues that must be considered include:

- Reliable power
- Transmission speeds
- Software availability
- Prevalence of software pirating

Any of these issues could affect the reliability and effectiveness of a GIS.

GIS ROLE SUBSIDIARY MANAGERS PLAY

In an MNC, subsidiaries must be efficiently managed in order for all operations to be successful, including establishing a GIS throughout the company. Challenges related to subsidiaries and how they are managed include:

- Managers want to be too independent
- Managers are focused solely on profitability
- Managers resent or do not wholly understand the GIS and its role

The support of managers in the subsidiary companies is vital to a successful GIS. How to maintain a good relationship with subsidiaries and help them overcome challenges that could limit the scope of the GIS should be included in an MNC's strategic planning.

Copyright © Mometrix Media. You have been licensed one copy of this document for personal use only. Any other reproduction or redistribution is strictly prohibited. All rights reserved.
This content is provided for test preparation purposes only and does not imply an endorsement by Mometrix of any particular political, scientific, or religious point of view.

DSST Practice Test

Want to take this practice test in an online interactive format?
Check out the online resources page, which includes interactive practice questions and much more: **mometrix.com/resources719/dsstmis**

1. Which type of office application software is best used for tracking an employee's expenses on a business trip?

a. Word processor
b. Spreadsheet
c. Database management system
d. Presentation software
e. Image editor

2. Which type of office application software is best used for making and maintaining an internal department newsletter to be printed and posted on a bulletin board?

a. Word processor
b. Spreadsheet
c. Database management system
d. Presentation software
e. Image editor

3. Which type of office application software is best used for keeping track of large amounts of data and generating reports on these data for training office employees in different departments, using various training materials?

a. Word processor
b. Spreadsheet
c. Database management system
d. Presentation software
e. Image editor

4. Items that appear on the desktop of a computer that start applications in other locations on the computer are called:

a. Wallpaper
b. Software
c. Operating system application tools
d. Shortcuts
e. Recycle bin

5. A file that is deleted from the computer ends up in the:

a. Wallpaper
b. software
c. operating system application tools
d. shortcuts
e. recycle bin

Copyright © Mometrix Media. You have been licensed one copy of this document for personal use only. Any other reproduction or redistribution is strictly prohibited. All rights reserved.
This content is provided for test preparation purposes only and does not imply an endorsement by Mometrix of any particular political, scientific, or religious point of view.

6. The image that appears as background on the desktop, behind any running applications, is called the:

a. Wallpaper
b. Software
c. Operating system application tools
d. Shortcuts
e. Recycle bin

7. All valid e-mail addresses must contain which of the following characters?

a. Space
b. Ampersand (&)
c. Dot (.)
d. Exclamation point (!)
e. At sign (@)

8. A valid e-mail address cannot contain which of the following characters?

a. Space
b. Ampersand (&)
c. Dot (.)
d. Exclamation point (!)
e. At sign (@)

9. Which of the following applications cannot be used to send and read e-mail?

a. Microsoft Outlook
b. Google Chrome
c. Terminal Window
d. Windows Mail
e. Spreadsheet

10. Which of the following applications is not a web browser?

a. Internet Explorer.
b. Firefox
c. Opera
d. Browsezilla
e. Safari

Copyright © Mometrix Media. You have been licensed one copy of this document for personal use only. Any other reproduction or redistribution is strictly prohibited. All rights reserved.
This content is provided for test preparation purposes only and does not imply an endorsement by Mometrix of any particular political, scientific, or religious point of view.

Answer Key and Explanations

1. B: Spreadsheet. Spreadsheet software is designed to do calculations and reports based on numerical calculations. The word processor software is used primarily for documents that include large amounts of text, such as memos and newsletters. Database management system software is used to track data and generate reports. Presentation software is used to show data to a group of people. An image editor is used to process, change, and edit graphical files.

2. A: Word processor. The word processor software is designed to process large amounts of text and enable the user to format and layout the text in a way that provides for detailed printing. Spreadsheet software is used for calculations and reporting on the calculations. Database management software is used to track data and generate reports on these data. Presentation software is designed to show data to a group of people. An image editor is used to process, change, and edit graphical files.

3. C: Database management system. Database management system software is designed to track large amounts of data and generate reports based on these data. Word processing software is designed to layout and format text. Spreadsheets are used to do mathematical calculations and reports based on these calculations. Presentation software is used to show data to a group of people. An image editor is used to process, change, and edit graphical files.

4. D: Shortcuts. Shortcuts appear on the desktop to allow the user easy access to start an application. These shortcuts can be added to and removed from the desktop without actually adding or removing the application on the computer. Wallpaper is the image that appears on the background of the desktop. These images can be selected from those provided with the operating system or can be downloaded to the computer to be used as wallpaper. Software describes any of the computer codes that are stored on the disc, such as applications and the operating system. The recycle bin stores applications and files that have been deleted so the user can restore them if the deletion was accidental; however, once the recycle bin has been emptied, the files are gone forever.

5. E: Recycle bin. The recycle bin stores applications and files that have been deleted so the user can restore them if the deletion was accidental; however, once the recycle bin has been emptied, the files are gone forever. Wallpaper is the image that appears on the background of the desktop. These images can be selected from those provided with the operating system or can be downloaded to the computer to be used as wallpaper. Software describes any of the computer codes that are stored on the disc, such as applications and the operating system. Shortcuts appear on the desktop to allow the user easy access to start an application. These shortcuts can be added to and removed from the desktop without actually adding or removing the application on the computer.

6. A: Wallpaper. Wallpaper is the image that appears on the background of the desktop. These images can be selected from those provided with the operating system or can be download to the computer to be used as wallpaper. Software describes any of the computer codes that are stored on the disc, such as applications and the operating system. Shortcuts allow the user easy access to start an application. These shortcuts can be added to and removed from the desktop without actually adding or removing the application on the computer. The recycle bin stores applications and files that have been deleted so the user can restore them if the deletion was accidental; however, once the recycle bin has been emptied, the files are gone forever.

7. E: @ sign. The @ sign is required in all e-mail addresses as part of the format for the e-mail address. This sign helps the Internet and mail processing computers to understand where to send

Copyright © Mometrix Media. You have been licensed one copy of this document for personal use only. Any other reproduction or redistribution is strictly prohibited. All rights reserved.
This content is provided for test preparation purposes only and does not imply an endorsement by Mometrix of any particular political, scientific, or religious point of view.

the e-mail. The part after the @ sign is the address of the computer that is the destination for the e-mail. The ampersand and explanation point can be included in e-mail addresses, but they are not commonly used. A dot is commonly used in e-mail addresses but is not required.

8. A: Space. A space is not allowed in any e-mail addresses. With Internet and mail processing computers, the space has a special meaning, but no e-mail address can contain a space. The ampersand and explanation point can be included in e-mail addresses, but they are not commonly used. A dot is commonly used in e-mail addresses but is not required. The @ sign is required in all e-mail addresses.

9. E: Spreadsheet. Spreadsheet applications are designed to do calculations and reports based on numerical calculations. Microsoft Outlook is the standard Microsoft application that is used to send and receive e-mail. Google Chrome is a web browser that allows you to browse the web and obtain e-mail via the Internet. A terminal window can be used to connect to an e-mail server and access e-mail accounts. Windows Mail is the application that is supplied with the Vista Operating System that is designed to send and receive e-mail.

10. D: Browsezilla. Browsezilla does not actually exist. Internet Explorer is Microsoft's version of the web browser. Firefox and Opera are popular open-source web browsers. Safari is the web browser used with Apple computers.

Copyright © Mometrix Media. You have been licensed one copy of this document for personal use only. Any other reproduction or redistribution is strictly prohibited. All rights reserved.
This content is provided for test preparation purposes only and does not imply an endorsement by Mometrix of any particular political, scientific, or religious point of view.

How to Overcome Test Anxiety

Just the thought of taking a test is enough to make most people a little nervous. A test is an important event that can have a long-term impact on your future, so it's important to take it seriously and it's natural to feel anxious about performing well. But just because anxiety is normal, that doesn't mean that it's helpful in test taking, or that you should simply accept it as part of your life. Anxiety can have a variety of effects. These effects can be mild, like making you feel slightly nervous, or severe, like blocking your ability to focus or remember even a simple detail.

If you experience test anxiety—whether severe or mild—it's important to know how to beat it. To discover this, first you need to understand what causes test anxiety.

Causes of Test Anxiety

While we often think of anxiety as an uncontrollable emotional state, it can actually be caused by simple, practical things. One of the most common causes of test anxiety is that a person does not feel adequately prepared for their test. This feeling can be the result of many different issues such as poor study habits or lack of organization, but the most common culprit is time management. Starting to study too late, failing to organize your study time to cover all of the material, or being distracted while you study will mean that you're not well prepared for the test. This may lead to cramming the night before, which will cause you to be physically and mentally exhausted for the test. Poor time management also contributes to feelings of stress, fear, and hopelessness as you realize you are not well prepared but don't know what to do about it.

Other times, test anxiety is not related to your preparation for the test but comes from unresolved fear. This may be a past failure on a test, or poor performance on tests in general. It may come from comparing yourself to others who seem to be performing better or from the stress of living up to expectations. Anxiety may be driven by fears of the future—how failure on this test would affect your educational and career goals. These fears are often completely irrational, but they can still negatively impact your test performance.

Elements of Test Anxiety

As mentioned earlier, test anxiety is considered to be an emotional state, but it has physical and mental components as well. Sometimes you may not even realize that you are suffering from test anxiety until you notice the physical symptoms. These can include trembling hands, rapid heartbeat, sweating, nausea, and tense muscles. Extreme anxiety may lead to fainting or vomiting. Obviously, any of these symptoms can have a negative impact on testing. It is important to recognize them as soon as they begin to occur so that you can address the problem before it damages your performance.

The mental components of test anxiety include trouble focusing and inability to remember learned information. During a test, your mind is on high alert, which can help you recall information and stay focused for an extended period of time. However, anxiety interferes with your mind's natural processes, causing you to blank out, even on the questions you know well. The strain of testing during anxiety makes it difficult to stay focused, especially on a test that may take several hours. Extreme anxiety can take a huge mental toll, making it difficult not only to recall test information but even to understand the test questions or pull your thoughts together.

Copyright © Mometrix Media. You have been licensed one copy of this document for personal use only. Any other reproduction or redistribution is strictly prohibited. All rights reserved.
This content is provided for test preparation purposes only and does not imply an endorsement by Mometrix of any particular political, scientific, or religious point of view.

Effects of Test Anxiety

Test anxiety is like a disease—if left untreated, it will get progressively worse. Anxiety leads to poor performance, and this reinforces the feelings of fear and failure, which in turn lead to poor performances on subsequent tests. It can grow from a mild nervousness to a crippling condition. If allowed to progress, test anxiety can have a big impact on your schooling, and consequently on your future.

Test anxiety can spread to other parts of your life. Anxiety on tests can become anxiety in any stressful situation, and blanking on a test can turn into panicking in a job situation. But fortunately, you don't have to let anxiety rule your testing and determine your grades. There are a number of relatively simple steps you can take to move past anxiety and function normally on a test and in the rest of life.

Physical Steps for Beating Test Anxiety

While test anxiety is a serious problem, the good news is that it can be overcome. It doesn't have to control your ability to think and remember information. While it may take time, you can begin taking steps today to beat anxiety.

Just as your first hint that you may be struggling with anxiety comes from the physical symptoms, the first step to treating it is also physical. Rest is crucial for having a clear, strong mind. If you are tired, it is much easier to give in to anxiety. But if you establish good sleep habits, your body and mind will be ready to perform optimally, without the strain of exhaustion. Additionally, sleeping well helps you to retain information better, so you're more likely to recall the answers when you see the test questions.

Getting good sleep means more than going to bed on time. It's important to allow your brain time to relax. Take study breaks from time to time so it doesn't get overworked, and don't study right before bed. Take time to rest your mind before trying to rest your body, or you may find it difficult to fall asleep.

Along with sleep, other aspects of physical health are important in preparing for a test. Good nutrition is vital for good brain function. Sugary foods and drinks may give a burst of energy but this burst is followed by a crash, both physically and emotionally. Instead, fuel your body with protein and vitamin-rich foods.

Also, drink plenty of water. Dehydration can lead to headaches and exhaustion, especially if your brain is already under stress from the rigors of the test. Particularly if your test is a long one, drink water during the breaks. And if possible, take an energy-boosting snack to eat between sections.

Along with sleep and diet, a third important part of physical health is exercise. Maintaining a steady workout schedule is helpful, but even taking 5-minute study breaks to walk can help get your blood pumping faster and clear your head. Exercise also releases endorphins, which contribute to a positive feeling and can help combat test anxiety.

When you nurture your physical health, you are also contributing to your mental health. If your body is healthy, your mind is much more likely to be healthy as well. So take time to rest, nourish your body with healthy food and water, and get moving as much as possible. Taking these physical steps will make you stronger and more able to take the mental steps necessary to overcome test anxiety.

Copyright © Mometrix Media. You have been licensed one copy of this document for personal use only. Any other reproduction or redistribution is strictly prohibited. All rights reserved.
This content is provided for test preparation purposes only and does not imply an endorsement by Mometrix of any particular political, scientific, or religious point of view.

Mental Steps for Beating Test Anxiety

Working on the mental side of test anxiety can be more challenging, but as with the physical side, there are clear steps you can take to overcome it. As mentioned earlier, test anxiety often stems from lack of preparation, so the obvious solution is to prepare for the test. Effective studying may be the most important weapon you have for beating test anxiety, but you can and should employ several other mental tools to combat fear.

First, boost your confidence by reminding yourself of past success—tests or projects that you aced. If you're putting as much effort into preparing for this test as you did for those, there's no reason you should expect to fail here. Work hard to prepare; then trust your preparation.

Second, surround yourself with encouraging people. It can be helpful to find a study group, but be sure that the people you're around will encourage a positive attitude. If you spend time with others who are anxious or cynical, this will only contribute to your own anxiety. Look for others who are motivated to study hard from a desire to succeed, not from a fear of failure.

Third, reward yourself. A test is physically and mentally tiring, even without anxiety, and it can be helpful to have something to look forward to. Plan an activity following the test, regardless of the outcome, such as going to a movie or getting ice cream.

When you are taking the test, if you find yourself beginning to feel anxious, remind yourself that you know the material. Visualize successfully completing the test. Then take a few deep, relaxing breaths and return to it. Work through the questions carefully but with confidence, knowing that you are capable of succeeding.

Developing a healthy mental approach to test taking will also aid in other areas of life. Test anxiety affects more than just the actual test—it can be damaging to your mental health and even contribute to depression. It's important to beat test anxiety before it becomes a problem for more than testing.

Study Strategy

Being prepared for the test is necessary to combat anxiety, but what does being prepared look like? You may study for hours on end and still not feel prepared. What you need is a strategy for test prep. The next few pages outline our recommended steps to help you plan out and conquer the challenge of preparation.

Step 1: Scope Out the Test

Learn everything you can about the format (multiple choice, essay, etc.) and what will be on the test. Gather any study materials, course outlines, or sample exams that may be available. Not only will this help you to prepare, but knowing what to expect can help to alleviate test anxiety.

Step 2: Map Out the Material

Look through the textbook or study guide and make note of how many chapters or sections it has. Then divide these over the time you have. For example, if a book has 15 chapters and you have five days to study, you need to cover three chapters each day. Even better, if you have the time, leave an extra day at the end for overall review after you have gone through the material in depth.

If time is limited, you may need to prioritize the material. Look through it and make note of which sections you think you already have a good grasp on, and which need review. While you are studying, skim quickly through the familiar sections and take more time on the challenging parts.

Copyright © Mometrix Media. You have been licensed one copy of this document for personal use only. Any other reproduction or redistribution is strictly prohibited. All rights reserved.
This content is provided for test preparation purposes only and does not imply an endorsement by Mometrix of any particular political, scientific, or religious point of view.

Write out your plan so you don't get lost as you go. Having a written plan also helps you feel more in control of the study, so anxiety is less likely to arise from feeling overwhelmed at the amount to cover.

Step 3: Gather Your Tools

Decide what study method works best for you. Do you prefer to highlight in the book as you study and then go back over the highlighted portions? Or do you type out notes of the important information? Or is it helpful to make flashcards that you can carry with you? Assemble the pens, index cards, highlighters, post-it notes, and any other materials you may need so you won't be distracted by getting up to find things while you study.

If you're having a hard time retaining the information or organizing your notes, experiment with different methods. For example, try color-coding by subject with colored pens, highlighters, or post-it notes. If you learn better by hearing, try recording yourself reading your notes so you can listen while in the car, working out, or simply sitting at your desk. Ask a friend to quiz you from your flashcards, or try teaching someone the material to solidify it in your mind.

Step 4: Create Your Environment

It's important to avoid distractions while you study. This includes both the obvious distractions like visitors and the subtle distractions like an uncomfortable chair (or a too-comfortable couch that makes you want to fall asleep). Set up the best study environment possible: good lighting and a comfortable work area. If background music helps you focus, you may want to turn it on, but otherwise keep the room quiet. If you are using a computer to take notes, be sure you don't have any other windows open, especially applications like social media, games, or anything else that could distract you. Silence your phone and turn off notifications. Be sure to keep water close by so you stay hydrated while you study (but avoid unhealthy drinks and snacks).

Also, take into account the best time of day to study. Are you freshest first thing in the morning? Try to set aside some time then to work through the material. Is your mind clearer in the afternoon or evening? Schedule your study session then. Another method is to study at the same time of day that you will take the test, so that your brain gets used to working on the material at that time and will be ready to focus at test time.

Step 5: Study!

Once you have done all the study preparation, it's time to settle into the actual studying. Sit down, take a few moments to settle your mind so you can focus, and begin to follow your study plan. Don't give in to distractions or let yourself procrastinate. This is your time to prepare so you'll be ready to fearlessly approach the test. Make the most of the time and stay focused.

Of course, you don't want to burn out. If you study too long you may find that you're not retaining the information very well. Take regular study breaks. For example, taking five minutes out of every hour to walk briskly, breathing deeply and swinging your arms, can help your mind stay fresh.

As you get to the end of each chapter or section, it's a good idea to do a quick review. Remind yourself of what you learned and work on any difficult parts. When you feel that you've mastered the material, move on to the next part. At the end of your study session, briefly skim through your notes again.

But while review is helpful, cramming last minute is NOT. If at all possible, work ahead so that you won't need to fit all your study into the last day. Cramming overloads your brain with more information than it can process and retain, and your tired mind may struggle to recall even

Copyright © Mometrix Media. You have been licensed one copy of this document for personal use only. Any other reproduction or redistribution is strictly prohibited. All rights reserved.
This content is provided for test preparation purposes only and does not imply an endorsement by Mometrix of any particular political, scientific, or religious point of view.

previously learned information when it is overwhelmed with last-minute study. Also, the urgent nature of cramming and the stress placed on your brain contribute to anxiety. You'll be more likely to go to the test feeling unprepared and having trouble thinking clearly.

So don't cram, and don't stay up late before the test, even just to review your notes at a leisurely pace. Your brain needs rest more than it needs to go over the information again. In fact, plan to finish your studies by noon or early afternoon the day before the test. Give your brain the rest of the day to relax or focus on other things, and get a good night's sleep. Then you will be fresh for the test and better able to recall what you've studied.

STEP 6: TAKE A PRACTICE TEST

Many courses offer sample tests, either online or in the study materials. This is an excellent resource to check whether you have mastered the material, as well as to prepare for the test format and environment.

Check the test format ahead of time: the number of questions, the type (multiple choice, free response, etc.), and the time limit. Then create a plan for working through them. For example, if you have 30 minutes to take a 60-question test, your limit is 30 seconds per question. Spend less time on the questions you know well so that you can take more time on the difficult ones.

If you have time to take several practice tests, take the first one open book, with no time limit. Work through the questions at your own pace and make sure you fully understand them. Gradually work up to taking a test under test conditions: sit at a desk with all study materials put away and set a timer. Pace yourself to make sure you finish the test with time to spare and go back to check your answers if you have time.

After each test, check your answers. On the questions you missed, be sure you understand why you missed them. Did you misread the question (tests can use tricky wording)? Did you forget the information? Or was it something you hadn't learned? Go back and study any shaky areas that the practice tests reveal.

Taking these tests not only helps with your grade, but also aids in combating test anxiety. If you're already used to the test conditions, you're less likely to worry about it, and working through tests until you're scoring well gives you a confidence boost. Go through the practice tests until you feel comfortable, and then you can go into the test knowing that you're ready for it.

Test Tips

On test day, you should be confident, knowing that you've prepared well and are ready to answer the questions. But aside from preparation, there are several test day strategies you can employ to maximize your performance.

First, as stated before, get a good night's sleep the night before the test (and for several nights before that, if possible). Go into the test with a fresh, alert mind rather than staying up late to study.

Try not to change too much about your normal routine on the day of the test. It's important to eat a nutritious breakfast, but if you normally don't eat breakfast at all, consider eating just a protein bar. If you're a coffee drinker, go ahead and have your normal coffee. Just make sure you time it so that the caffeine doesn't wear off right in the middle of your test. Avoid sugary beverages, and drink enough water to stay hydrated but not so much that you need a restroom break 10 minutes into the

Copyright © Mometrix Media. You have been licensed one copy of this document for personal use only. Any other reproduction or redistribution is strictly prohibited. All rights reserved.
This content is provided for test preparation purposes only and does not imply an endorsement by Mometrix of any particular political, scientific, or religious point of view.

test. If your test isn't first thing in the morning, consider going for a walk or doing a light workout before the test to get your blood flowing.

Allow yourself enough time to get ready, and leave for the test with plenty of time to spare so you won't have the anxiety of scrambling to arrive in time. Another reason to be early is to select a good seat. It's helpful to sit away from doors and windows, which can be distracting. Find a good seat, get out your supplies, and settle your mind before the test begins.

When the test begins, start by going over the instructions carefully, even if you already know what to expect. Make sure you avoid any careless mistakes by following the directions.

Then begin working through the questions, pacing yourself as you've practiced. If you're not sure on an answer, don't spend too much time on it, and don't let it shake your confidence. Either skip it and come back later, or eliminate as many wrong answers as possible and guess among the remaining ones. Don't dwell on these questions as you continue—put them out of your mind and focus on what lies ahead.

Be sure to read all of the answer choices, even if you're sure the first one is the right answer. Sometimes you'll find a better one if you keep reading. But don't second-guess yourself if you do immediately know the answer. Your gut instinct is usually right. Don't let test anxiety rob you of the information you know.

If you have time at the end of the test (and if the test format allows), go back and review your answers. Be cautious about changing any, since your first instinct tends to be correct, but make sure you didn't misread any of the questions or accidentally mark the wrong answer choice. Look over any you skipped and make an educated guess.

At the end, leave the test feeling confident. You've done your best, so don't waste time worrying about your performance or wishing you could change anything. Instead, celebrate the successful completion of this test. And finally, use this test to learn how to deal with anxiety even better next time.

Review Video: Test Anxiety
Visit mometrix.com/academy and enter code: 100340

Important Qualification

Not all anxiety is created equal. If your test anxiety is causing major issues in your life beyond the classroom or testing center, or if you are experiencing troubling physical symptoms related to your anxiety, it may be a sign of a serious physiological or psychological condition. If this sounds like your situation, we strongly encourage you to seek professional help.

Copyright © Mometrix Media. You have been licensed one copy of this document for personal use only. Any other reproduction or redistribution is strictly prohibited. All rights reserved.
This content is provided for test preparation purposes only and does not imply an endorsement by Mometrix of any particular political, scientific, or religious point of view.

Thank You

We at Mometrix would like to extend our heartfelt thanks to you, our friend and patron, for allowing us to play a part in your journey. It is a privilege to serve people from all walks of life who are unified in their commitment to building the best future they can for themselves.

The preparation you devote to these important testing milestones may be the most valuable educational opportunity you have for making a real difference in your life. We encourage you to put your heart into it—that feeling of succeeding, overcoming, and yes, conquering will be well worth the hours you've invested.

We want to hear your story, your struggles and your successes, and if you see any opportunities for us to improve our materials so we can help others even more effectively in the future, please share that with us as well. **The team at Mometrix would be absolutely thrilled to hear from you!** So please, send us an email (support@mometrix.com) and let's stay in touch.

If you'd like some additional help, check out these other resources we offer for your exam:
http://MometrixFlashcards.com/DSST

Copyright © Mometrix Media. You have been licensed one copy of this document for personal use only. Any other reproduction or redistribution is strictly prohibited. All rights reserved.
This content is provided for test preparation purposes only and does not imply an endorsement by Mometrix of any particular political, scientific, or religious point of view.

Online Resources

Due to our efforts to try to keep this book to a manageable length, we've created a link that will give you access to all of your online resources:

mometrix.com/resources719/dsstmis

It's Your Moment, Let's Celebrate It!

Share your story @mometrixtestpreparation

Copyright © Mometrix Media. You have been licensed one copy of this document for personal use only. Any other reproduction or redistribution is strictly prohibited. All rights reserved.
This content is provided for test preparation purposes only and does not imply an endorsement by Mometrix of any particular political, scientific, or religious point of view.